D1282900

Courageous Kids

SYBIL LUDINGTON RIDES TO THE RESCUE

Courageous Kid of the American Revolution

by Jessica Gunderson

illustrated by Pablo Gallego

Consultant:
Richard Bell,
Associate Professor of History,
University of Maryland

CAPSTONE PRESS
a capstone imprint

Graphic Library is published by Capstone Press, an imprint of Capstone.

1710 Roe Crest Drive, North Mankato, Minnesota 56003

www.capstonepub.com

Library of Congress Cataloging-in-Publication Data

Names: Gunderson, Jessica, author.
Title: Sybil Ludington rides to the rescue : courageous kid of the American Revolution / by Jessica Gunderson.
Description: North Mankato : Capstone Press, [2021] | Series: Courageous kids | Includes bibliographical references and index. | Audience: Ages 8-9 | Audience: Grades 2-3 | Summary: "In 1777, the American Revolution is well underway. At 16, Sybil Ludington knows the war all too well. Her father is a colonel in the Continental Army, battling for America's independence from Great Britain. Colonel Ludington and his regiment are home for the season when word comes that the British Army is attacking nearby. It's up to young Sybil to alert the American militia that the British are coming."—Provided by publisher.
Identifiers: LCCN 2020003338 (print) | LCCN 2020003339 (ebook) | ISBN 9781496685032 (hardcover) | ISBN 9781496688040 (paperback) | ISBN 9781496685070 (pdf)
Subjects: LCSH: Ludington, Sybil, 1761—Juvenile literature. | Danbury (Conn.)—History—Burning by the British, 1777—Juvenile literature. | United States—History—Revolution, 1775-1783—Biography—Juvenile literature. | United States—History—Revolution, 1775-1783—Women—Juvenile literature.
Classification: LCC E241.D2 G86 2021 (print) | LCC E241.D2 (ebook) | DDC 973.3/33092 [B]—dc23
LC record available at https://lccn.loc.gov/2020003338
LC ebook record available at https://lccn.loc.gov/2020003339

EDITOR
Alison Deering

ART DIRECTOR
Nathan Gassman

DESIGNER
Ted Williams

MEDIA RESEARCHER
Morgan Walters

PRODUCTION SPECIALIST
Laura Manthe

Printed and bound in the United States of America.
PA117

TABLE OF CONTENTS

REVOLUTION BEGINS.....................4

CALL TO ARMS 10

A REVOLUTIONARY RIDE...............16

HOMECOMING...........................24

SYBIL LUDINGTON RIDES ON 28

GLOSSARY 30

READ MORE.............................31

INTERNET SITES 31

INDEX 32

REVOLUTION BEGINS

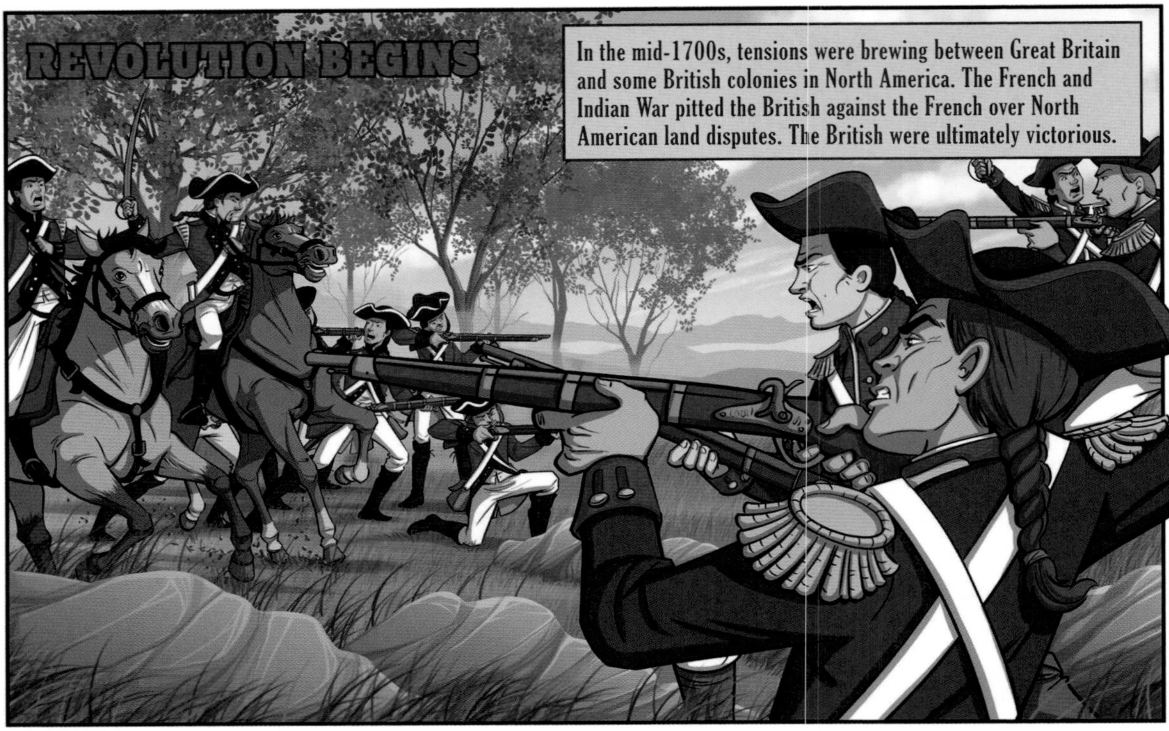
In the mid-1700s, tensions were brewing between Great Britain and some British colonies in North America. The French and Indian War pitted the British against the French over North American land disputes. The British were ultimately victorious.

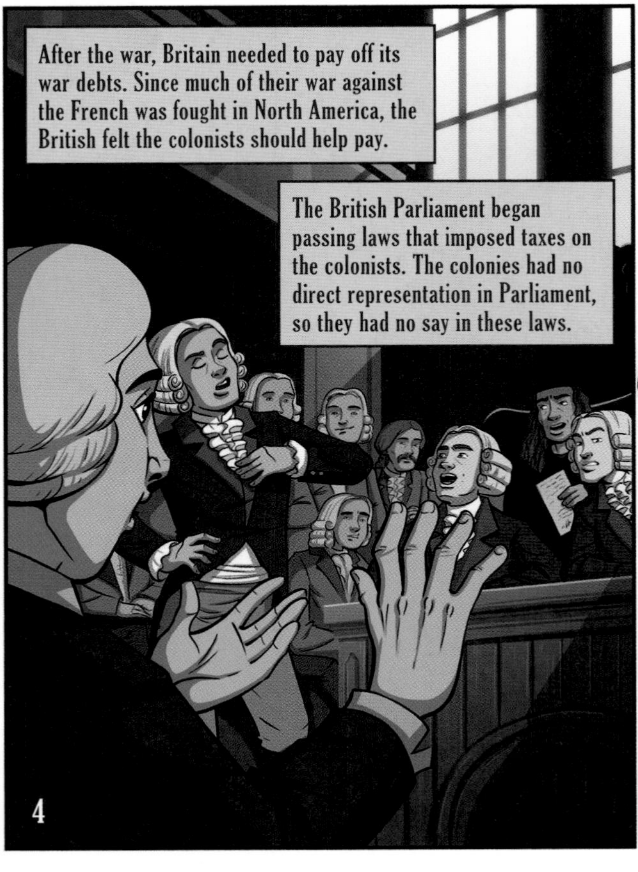
After the war, Britain needed to pay off its war debts. Since much of their war against the French was fought in North America, the British felt the colonists should help pay.
The British Parliament began passing laws that imposed taxes on the colonists. The colonies had no direct representation in Parliament, so they had no say in these laws.

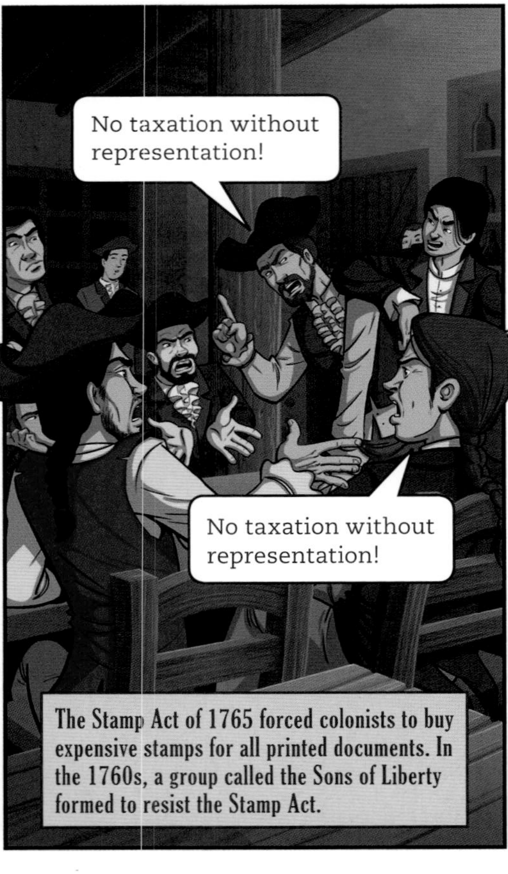
No taxation without representation!
No taxation without representation!
The Stamp Act of 1765 forced colonists to buy expensive stamps for all printed documents. In the 1760s, a group called the Sons of Liberty formed to resist the Stamp Act.

In 1773, angered by the terms of a new tax on tea, the Sons of Liberty destroyed a shipment of tea in Boston Harbor. The British responded by closing Boston's harbor and taking away the Massachusetts colony's right to self-govern.

This angered many colonists. They formed their own governing body, the Continental Congress. They also began forming militia groups made up of local citizens.

In April 1775, British troops marched toward Concord, Massachusetts, to seize colonial weapons and round up some patriot leaders. But the colonial militia intercepted them at Lexington. A shot was fired, and a battle ensued. The Battle of Lexington began the American Revolution.

On July 2, 1776, the Continental Congress voted in favor of independence from Great Britain. Two days later, it was made official with the proclamation of the Declaration of Independence.

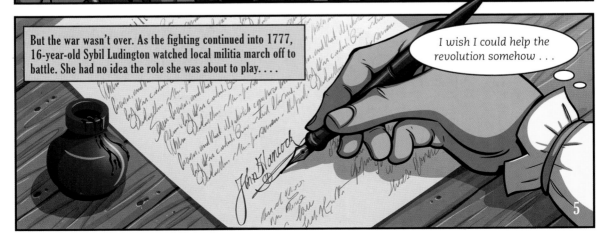

But the war wasn't over. As the fighting continued into 1777, 16-year-old Sybil Ludington watched local militia march off to battle. She had no idea the role she was about to play. . . .

I wish I could help the revolution somehow . . .

5

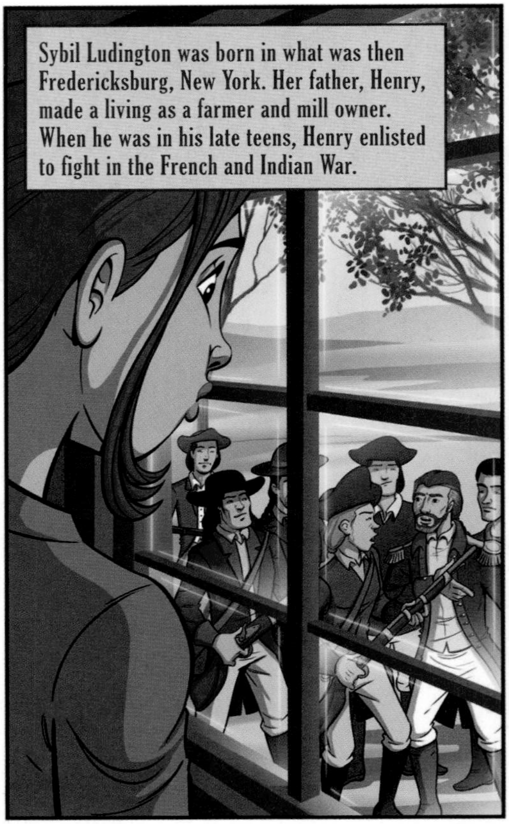
Sybil Ludington was born in what was then Fredericksburg, New York. Her father, Henry, made a living as a farmer and mill owner. When he was in his late teens, Henry enlisted to fight in the French and Indian War.

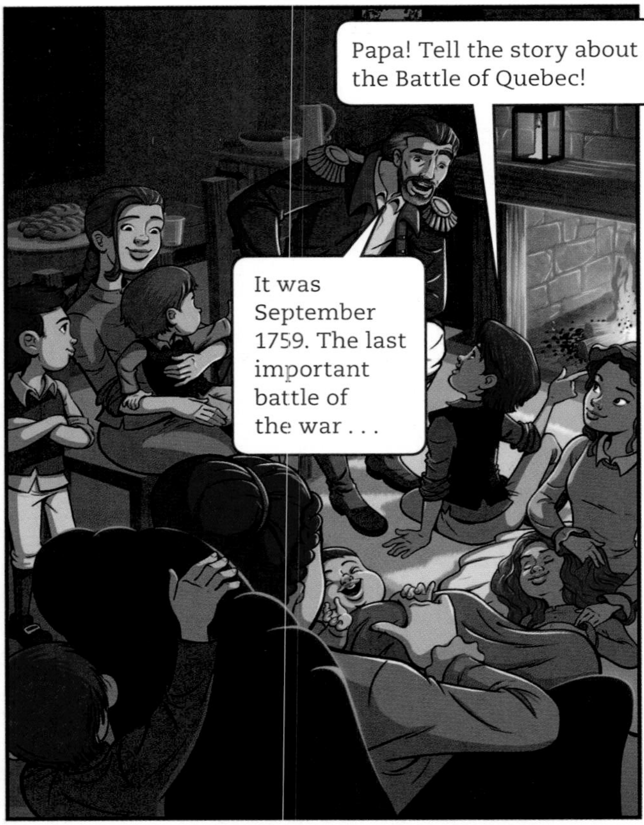
Papa! Tell the story about the Battle of Quebec!
It was September 1759. The last important battle of the war . . .

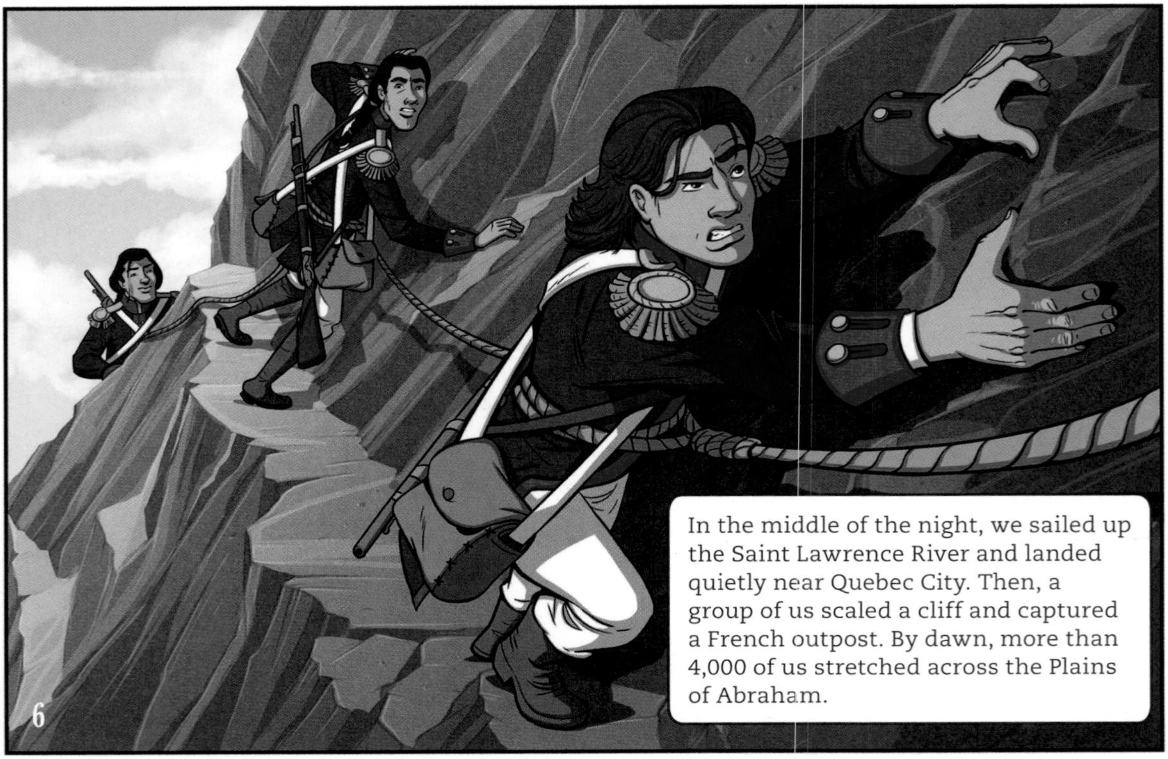
In the middle of the night, we sailed up the Saint Lawrence River and landed quietly near Quebec City. Then, a group of us scaled a cliff and captured a French outpost. By dawn, more than 4,000 of us stretched across the Plains of Abraham.

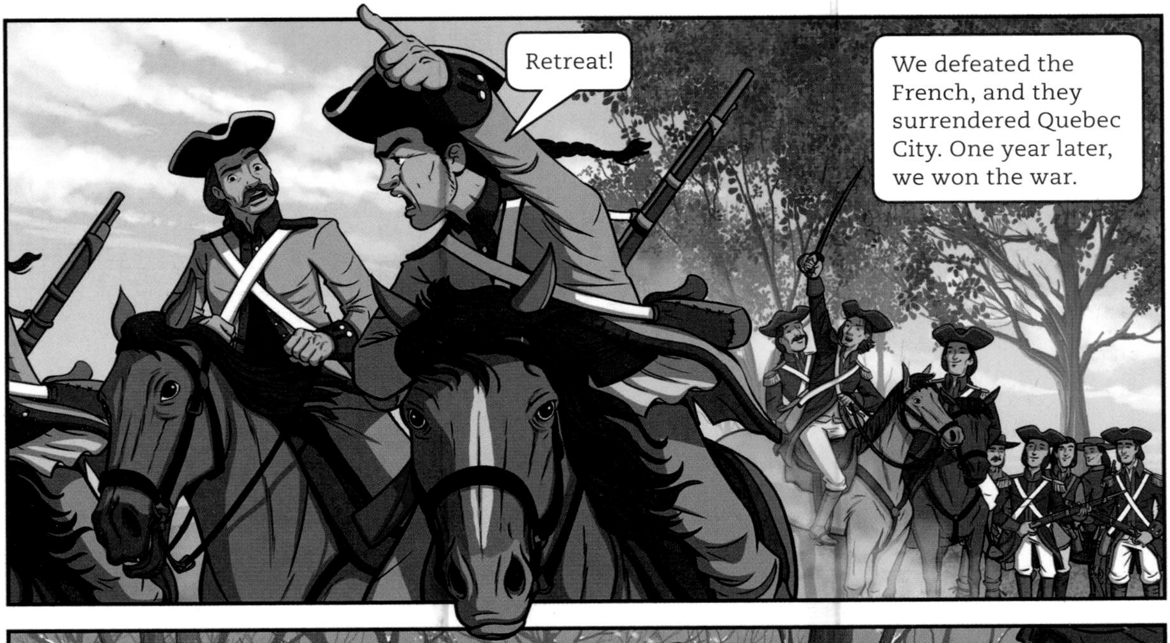
Retreat!
We defeated the French, and they surrendered Quebec City. One year later, we won the war.

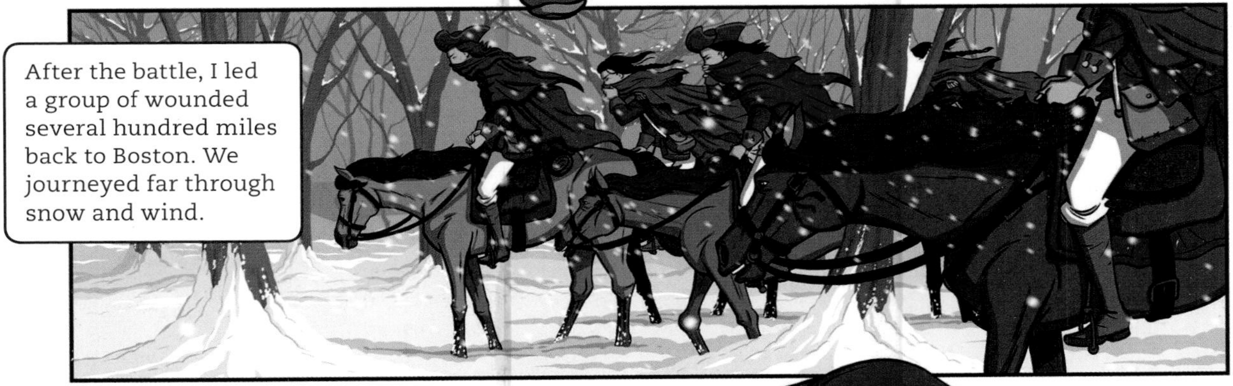
After the battle, I led a group of wounded several hundred miles back to Boston. We journeyed far through snow and wind.

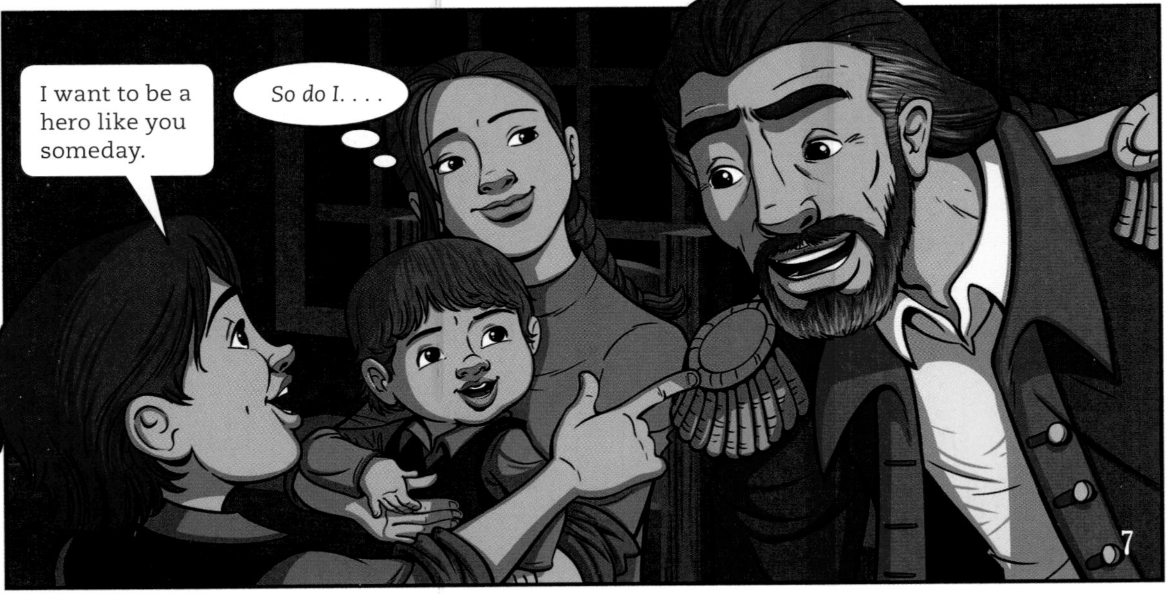
I want to be a hero like you someday.
So do I. . . .

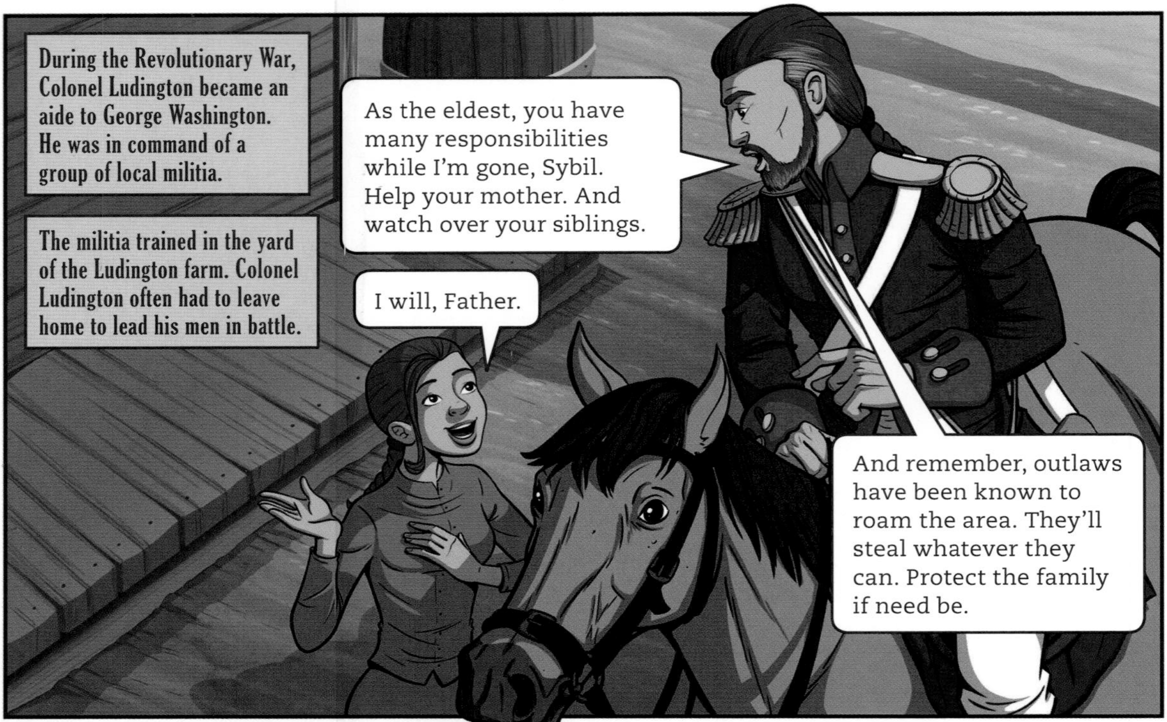
During the Revolutionary War, Colonel Ludington became an aide to George Washington. He was in command of a group of local militia.
The militia trained in the yard of the Ludington farm. Colonel Ludington often had to leave home to lead his men in battle.
As the eldest, you have many responsibilities while I'm gone, Sybil. Help your mother. And watch over your siblings.
I will, Father.
And remember, outlaws have been known to roam the area. They'll steal whatever they can. Protect the family if need be.

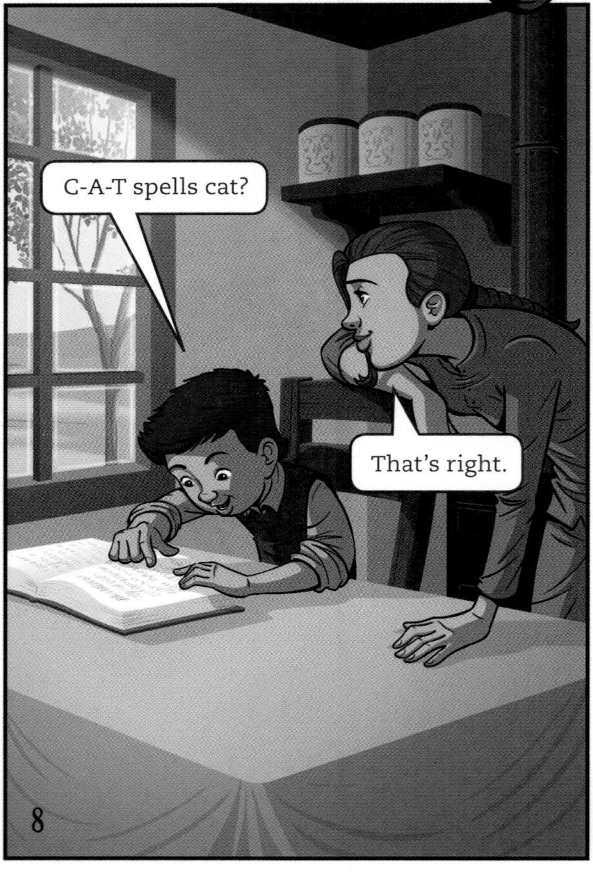
C-A-T spells cat?
That's right.

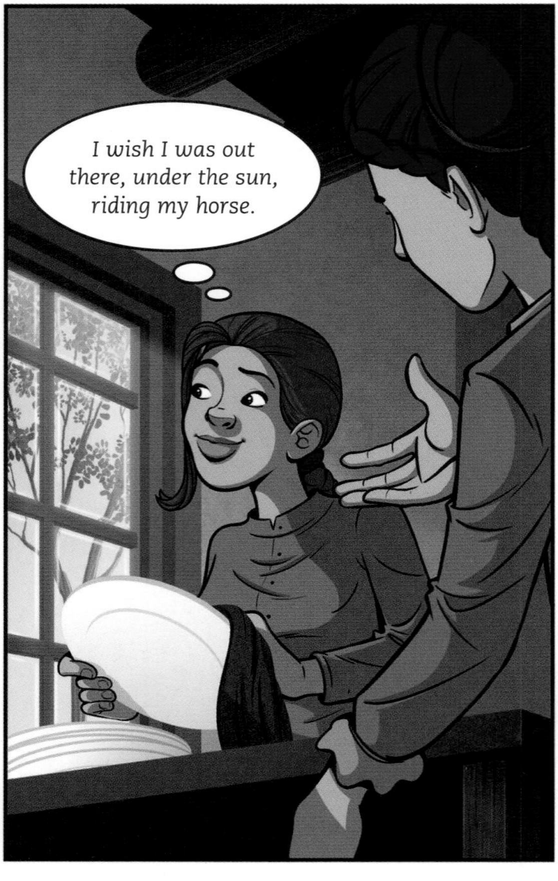
I wish I was out there, under the sun, riding my horse.

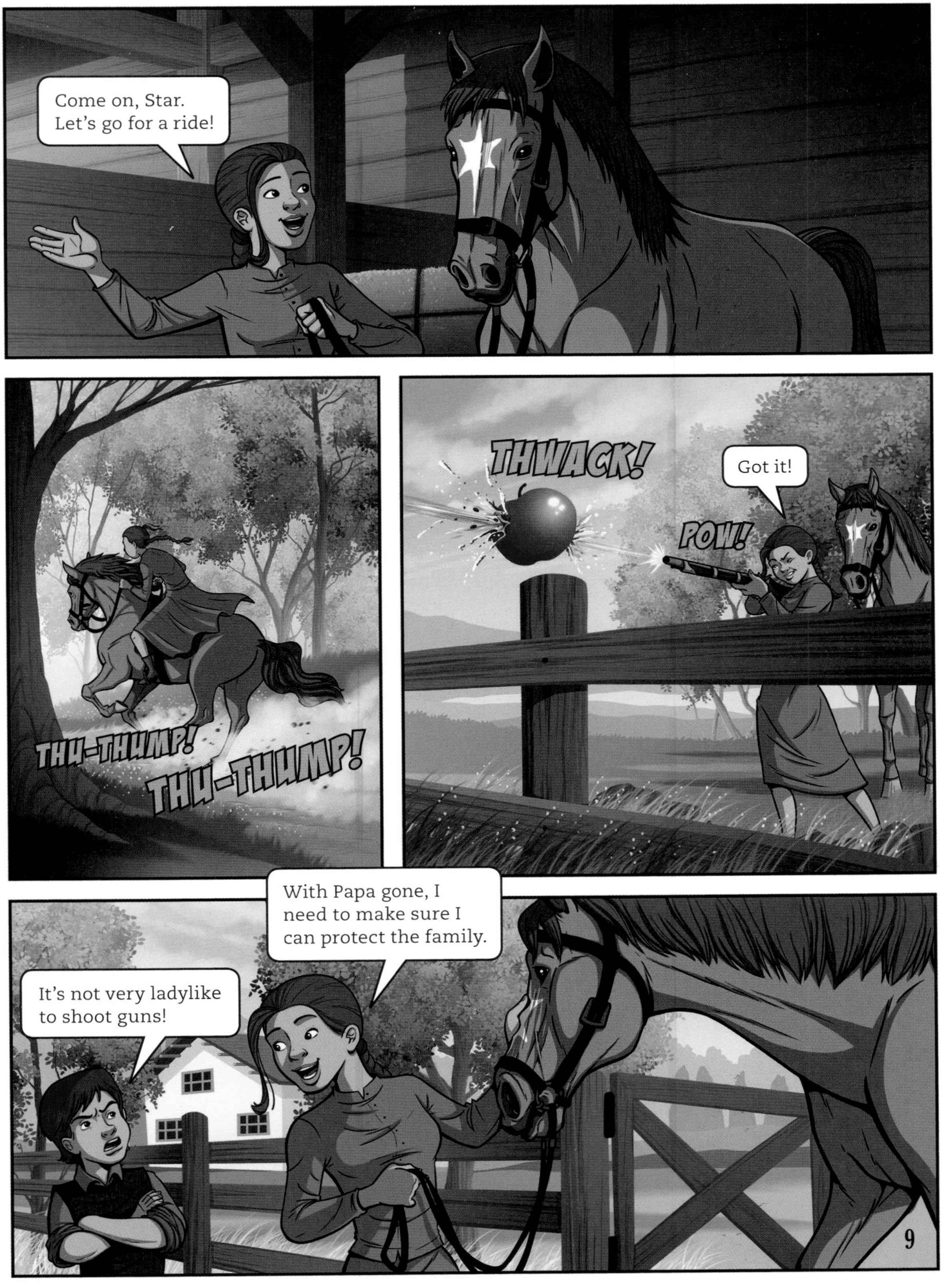
Come on, Star.
Let's go for a ride!
THU-THUMP!
THU-THUMP!
THWACK!
Got it!
POW!
With Papa gone, I need to make sure I can protect the family.
It's not very ladylike to shoot guns!

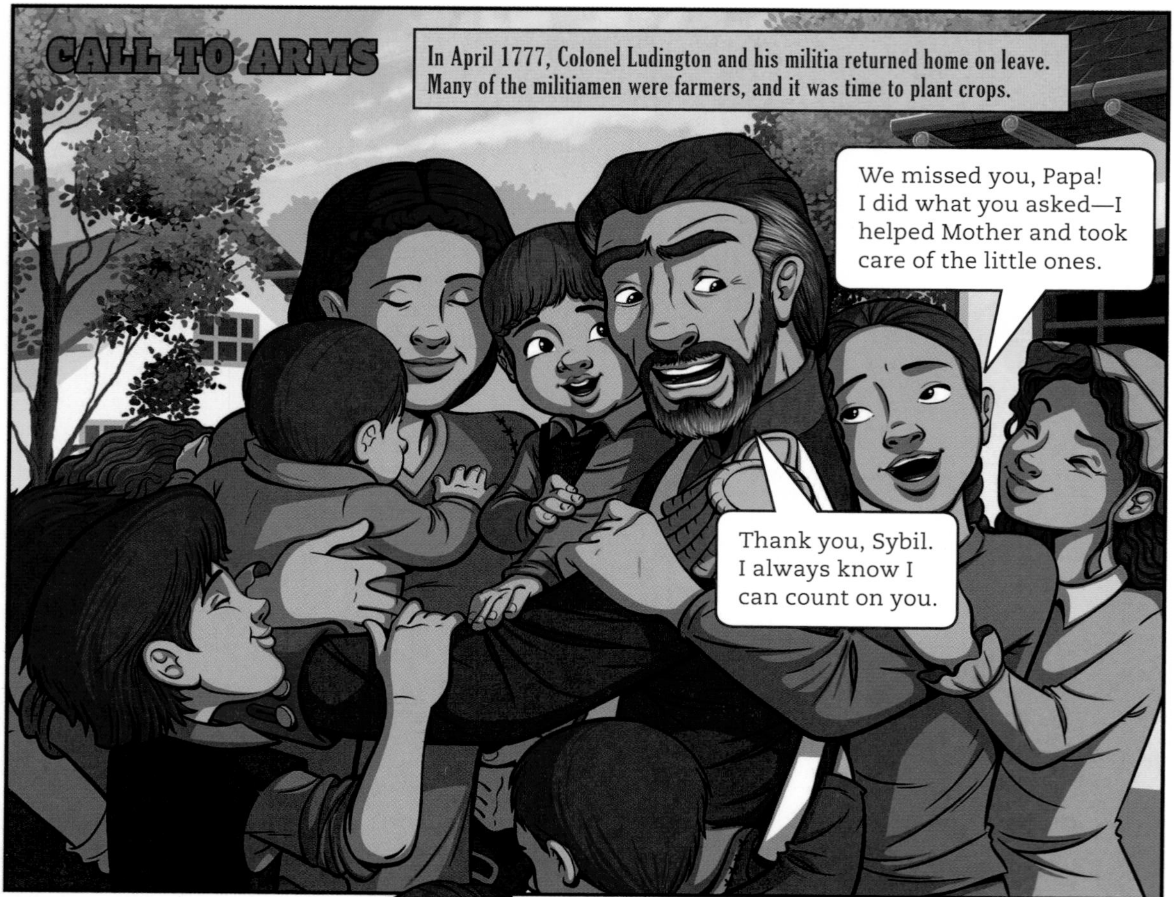
CALL TO ARMS
In April 1777, Colonel Ludington and his militia returned home on leave. Many of the militiamen were farmers, and it was time to plant crops.
We missed you, Papa! I did what you asked—I helped Mother and took care of the little ones.
Thank you, Sybil. I always know I can count on you.
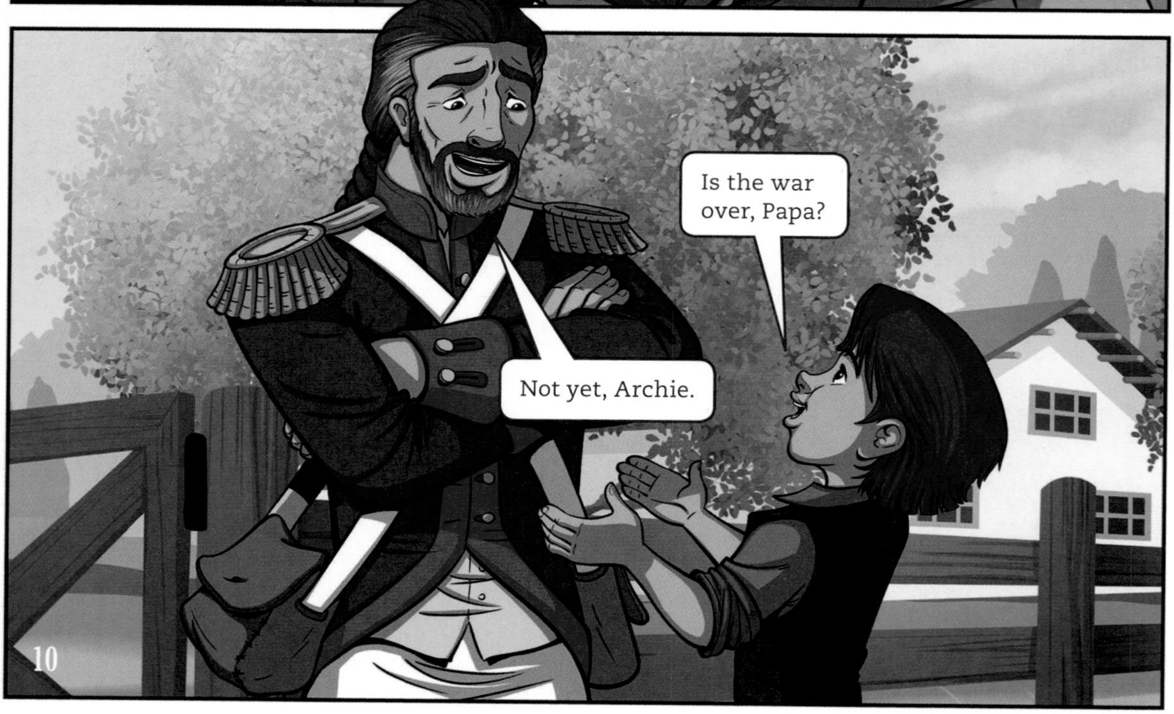
Is the war over, Papa?
Not yet, Archie.

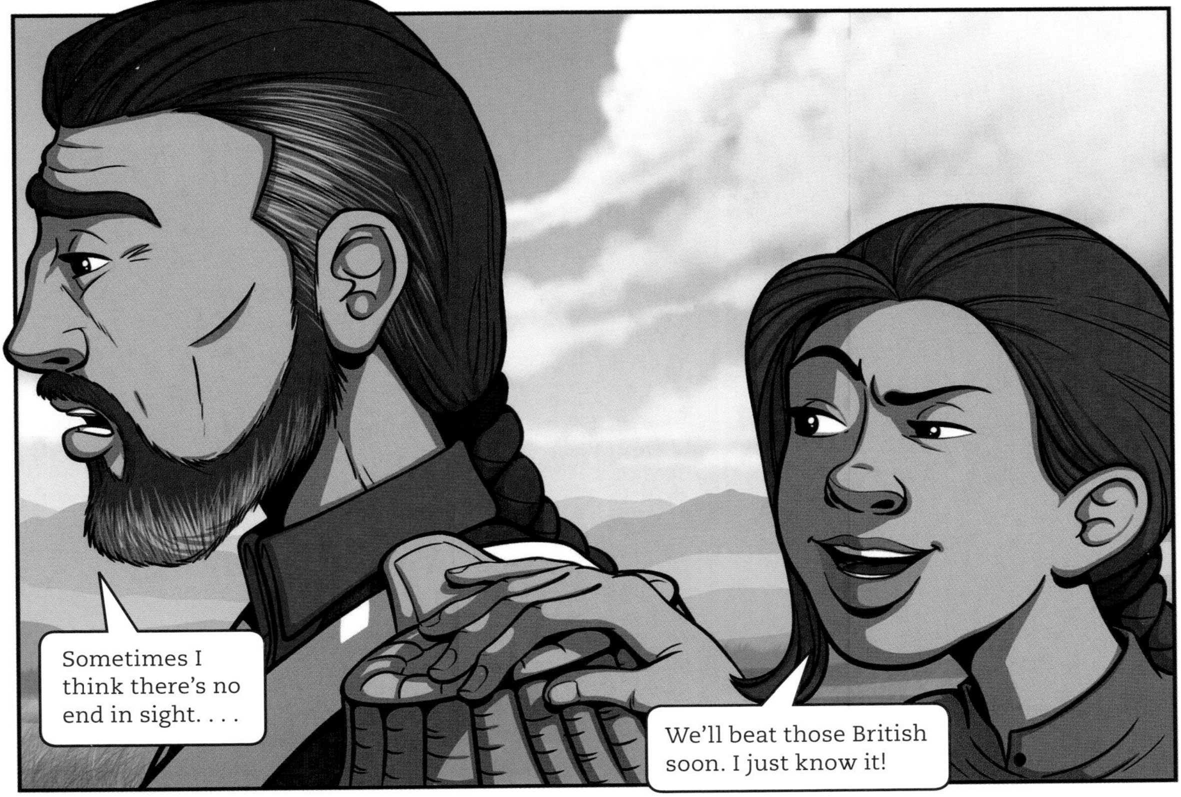
Sometimes I think there's no end in sight. . . .
We'll beat those British soon. I just know it!

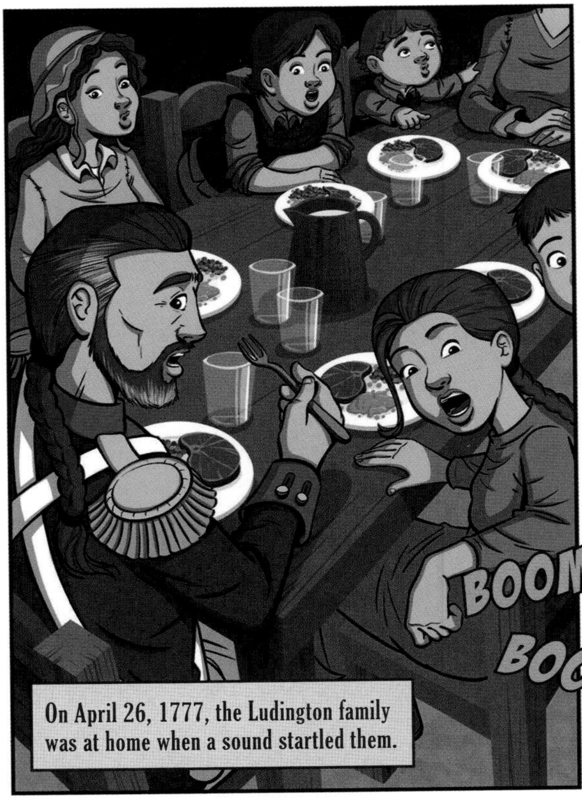
On April 26, 1777, the Ludington family was at home when a sound startled them.
BOOM!
BOOM!

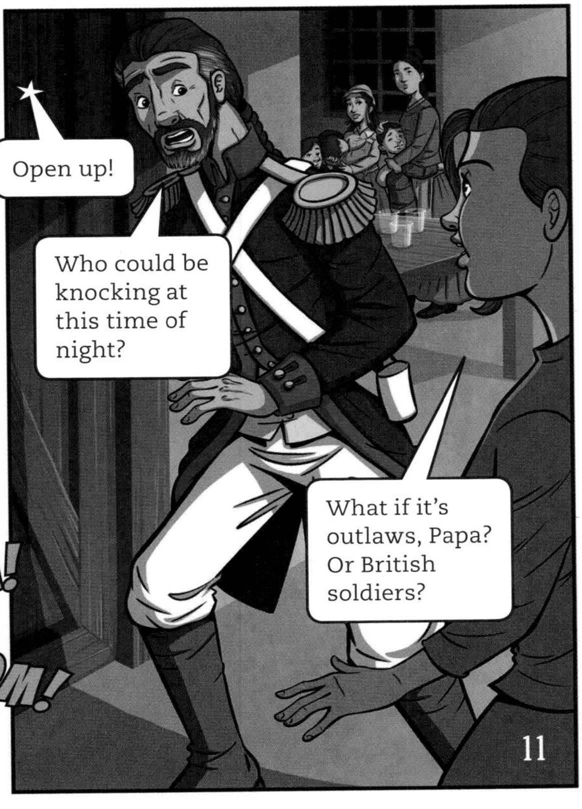
Open up!
Who could be knocking at this time of night?
What if it's outlaws, Papa? Or British soldiers?

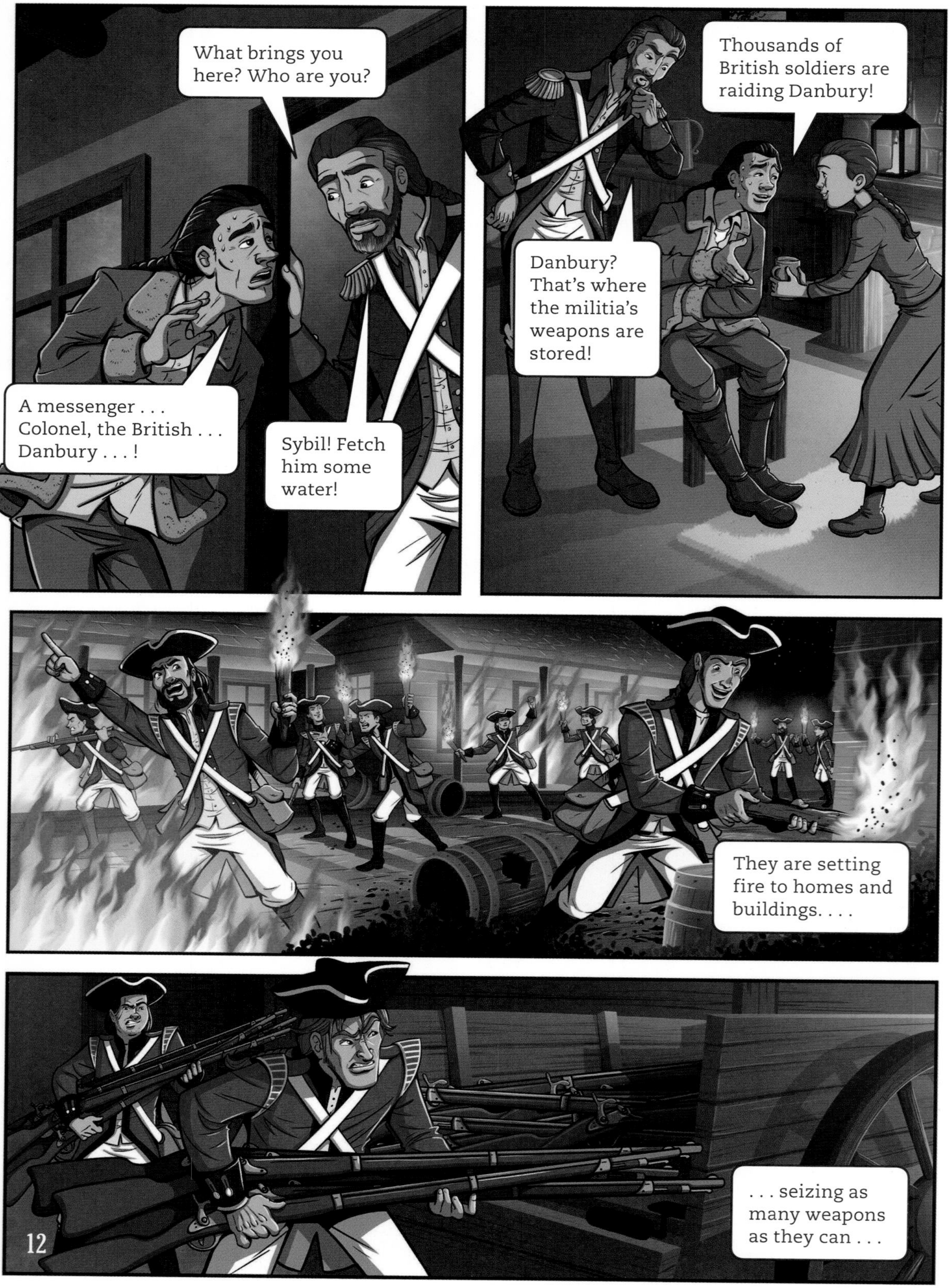
What brings you here? Who are you?
A messenger . . . Colonel, the British . . . Danbury . . . !
Sybil! Fetch him some water!
Thousands of British soldiers are raiding Danbury!
Danbury? That's where the militia's weapons are stored!
They are setting fire to homes and buildings. . . .
. . . seizing as many weapons as they can . . .

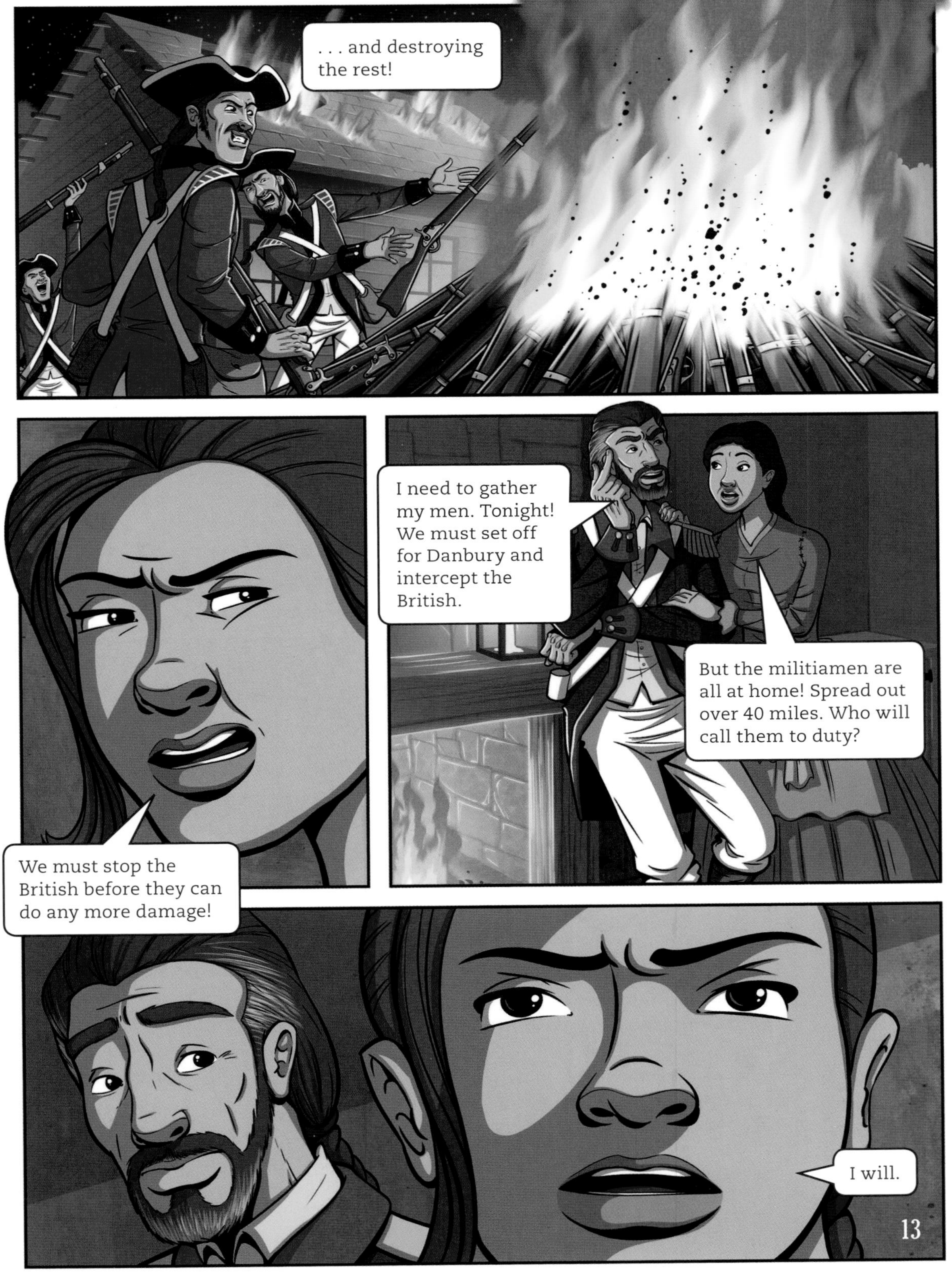
. . . and destroying the rest!
We must stop the British before they can do any more damage!
I need to gather my men. Tonight! We must set off for Danbury and intercept the British.
But the militiamen are all at home! Spread out over 40 miles. Who will call them to duty?
I will.

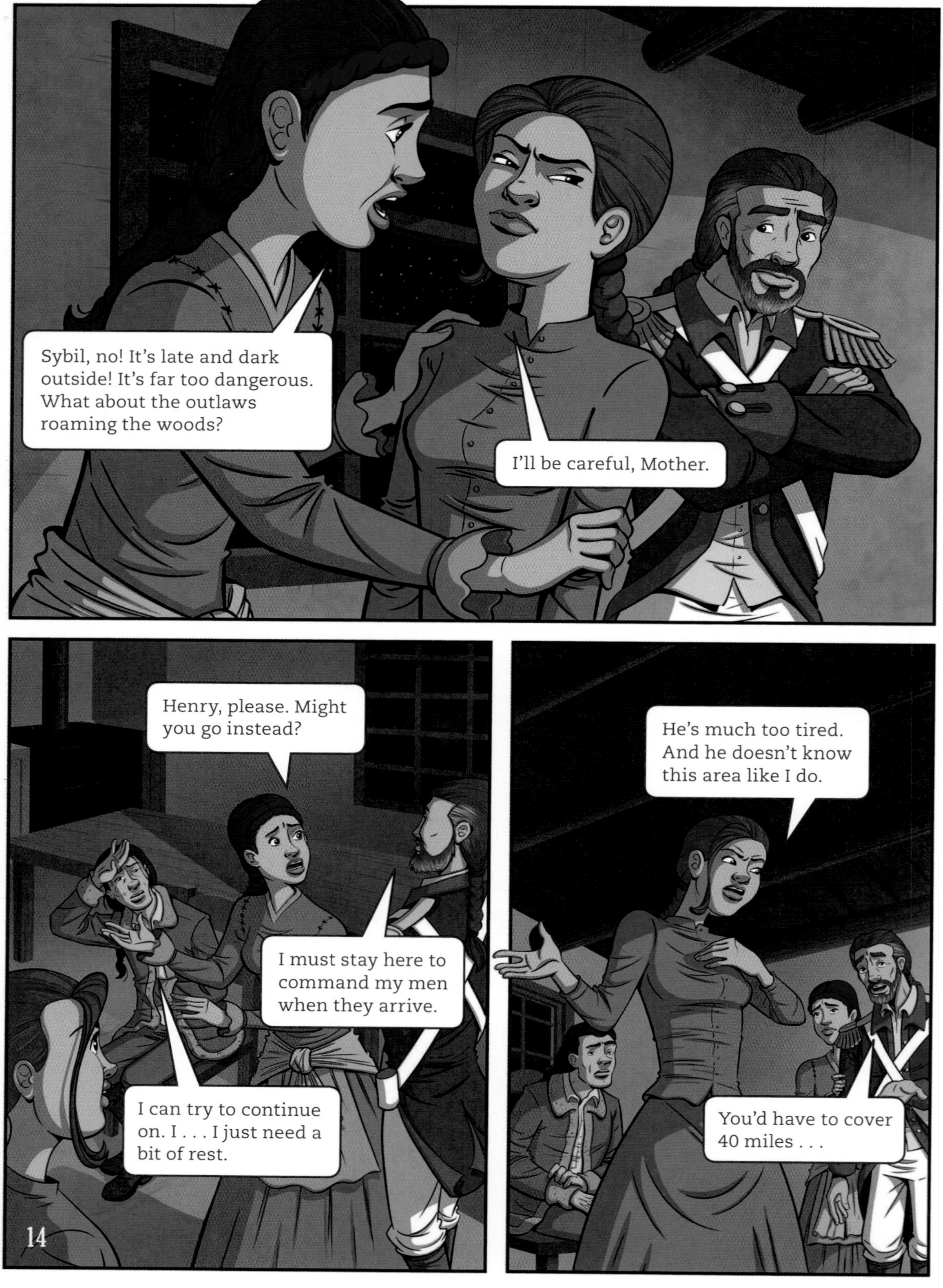
Sybil, no! It's late and dark outside! It's far too dangerous. What about the outlaws roaming the woods?
I'll be careful, Mother.
Henry, please. Might you go instead?
I must stay here to command my men when they arrive.
I can try to continue on. I . . . I just need a bit of rest.
He's much too tired. And he doesn't know this area like I do.
You'd have to cover 40 miles . . .

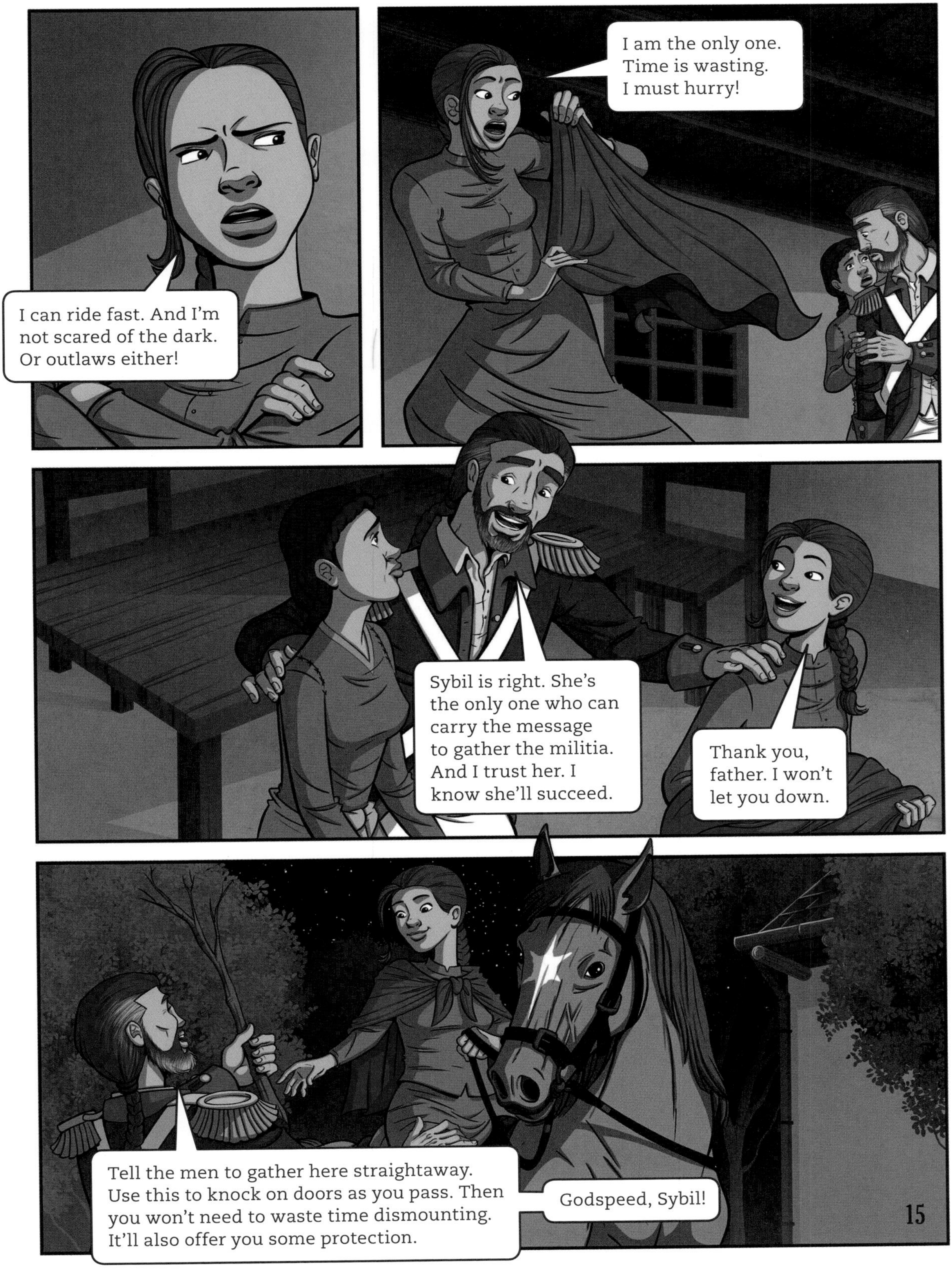
I can ride fast. And I'm not scared of the dark. Or outlaws either!
I am the only one. Time is wasting. I must hurry!
Sybil is right. She's the only one who can carry the message to gather the militia. And I trust her. I know she'll succeed.
Thank you, father. I won't let you down.
Tell the men to gather here straightaway. Use this to knock on doors as you pass. Then you won't need to waste time dismounting. It'll also offer you some protection.
Godspeed, Sybil!

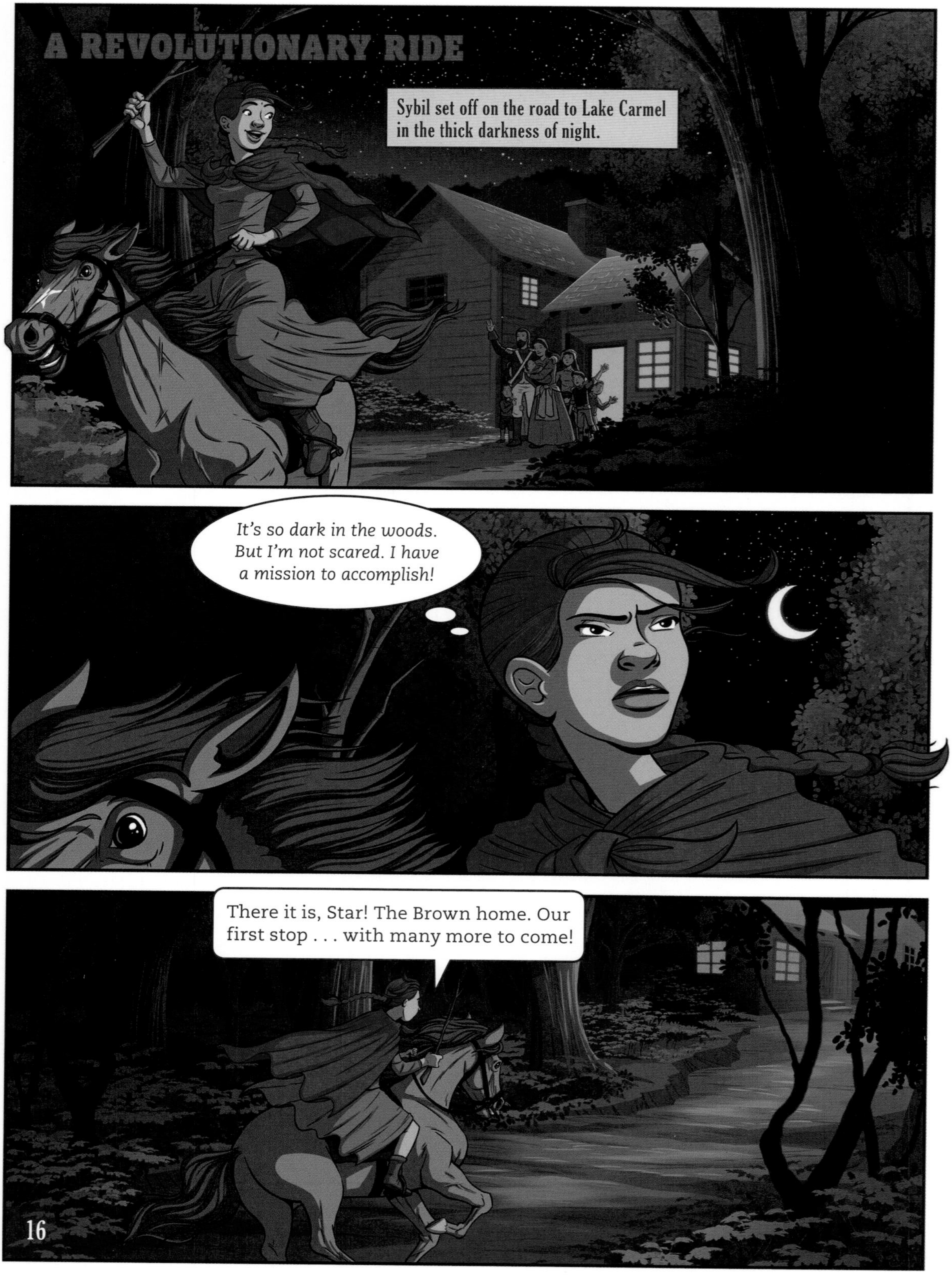
A REVOLUTIONARY RIDE
Sybil set off on the road to Lake Carmel in the thick darkness of night.
It's so dark in the woods. But I'm not scared. I have a mission to accomplish!
There it is, Star! The Brown home. Our first stop . . . with many more to come!

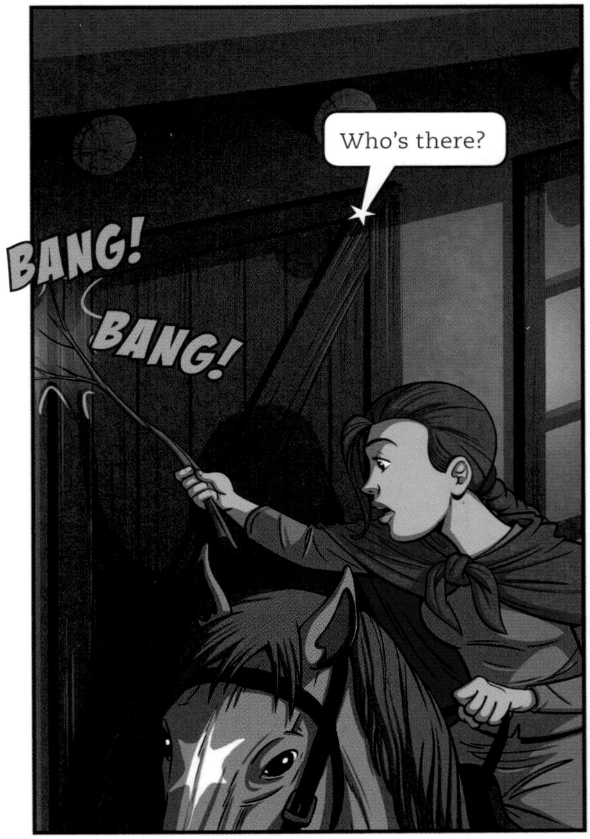
Who's there?
BANG!
BANG!

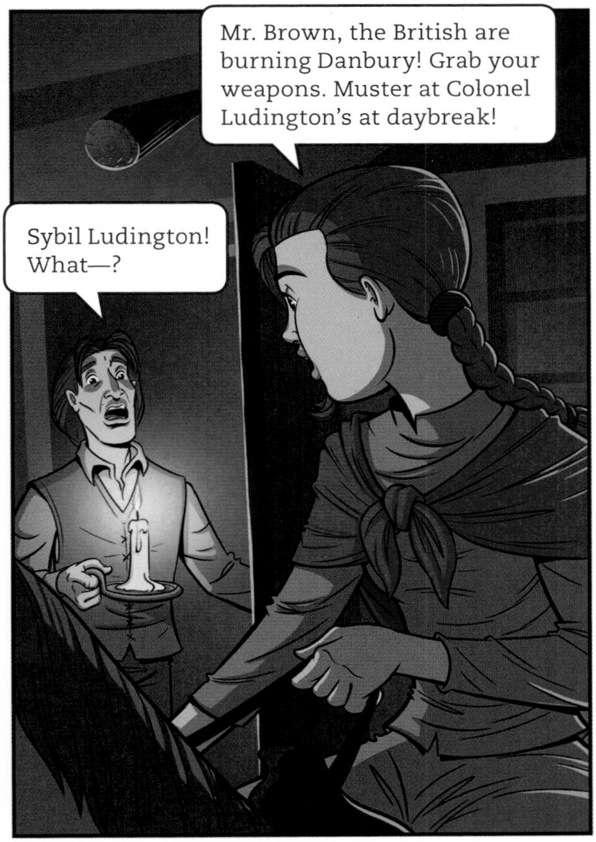
Mr. Brown, the British are burning Danbury! Grab your weapons. Muster at Colonel Ludington's at daybreak!
Sybil Ludington! What—?

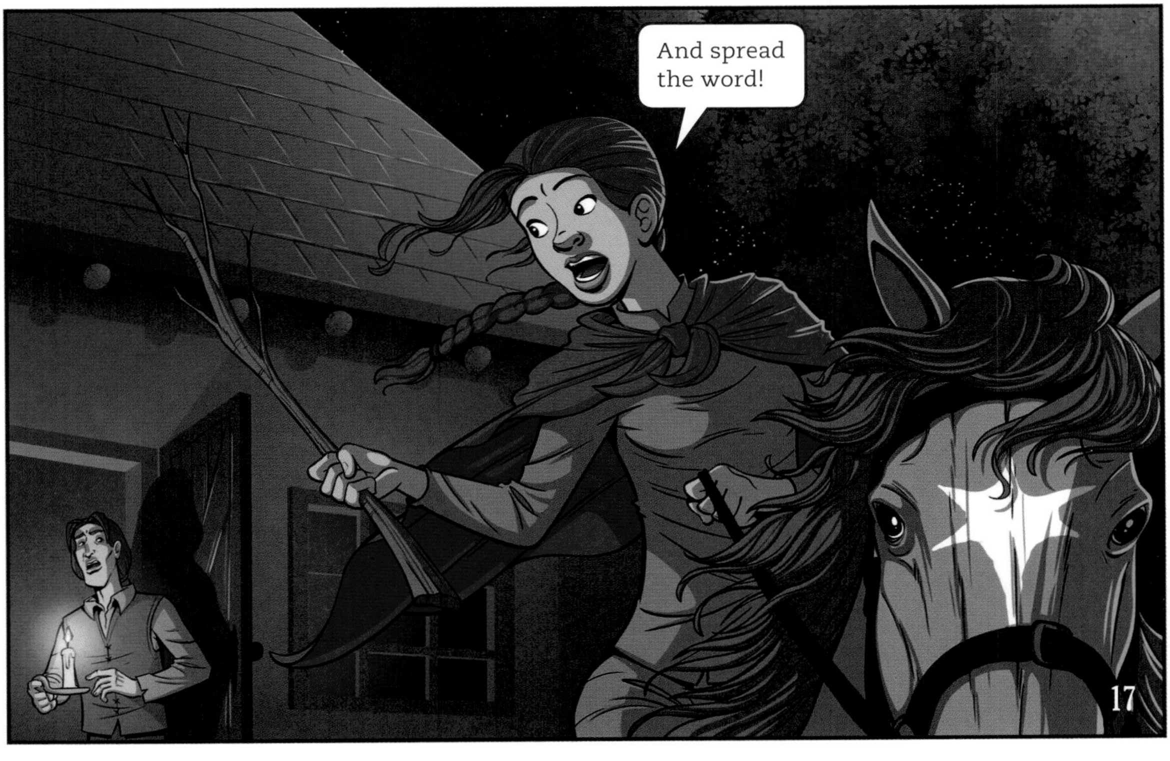
And spread the word!

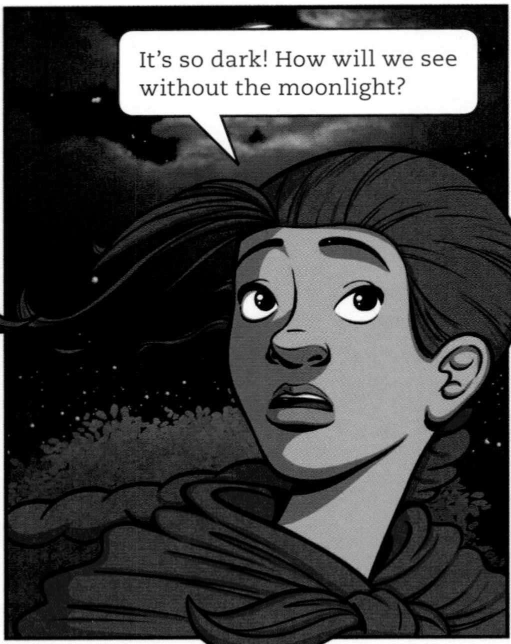
It's so dark! How will we see without the moonlight?

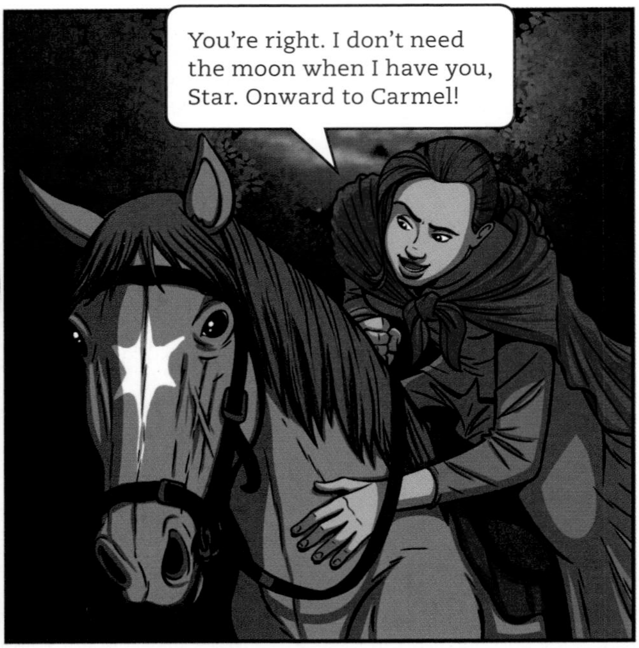
You're right. I don't need the moon when I have you, Star. Onward to Carmel!

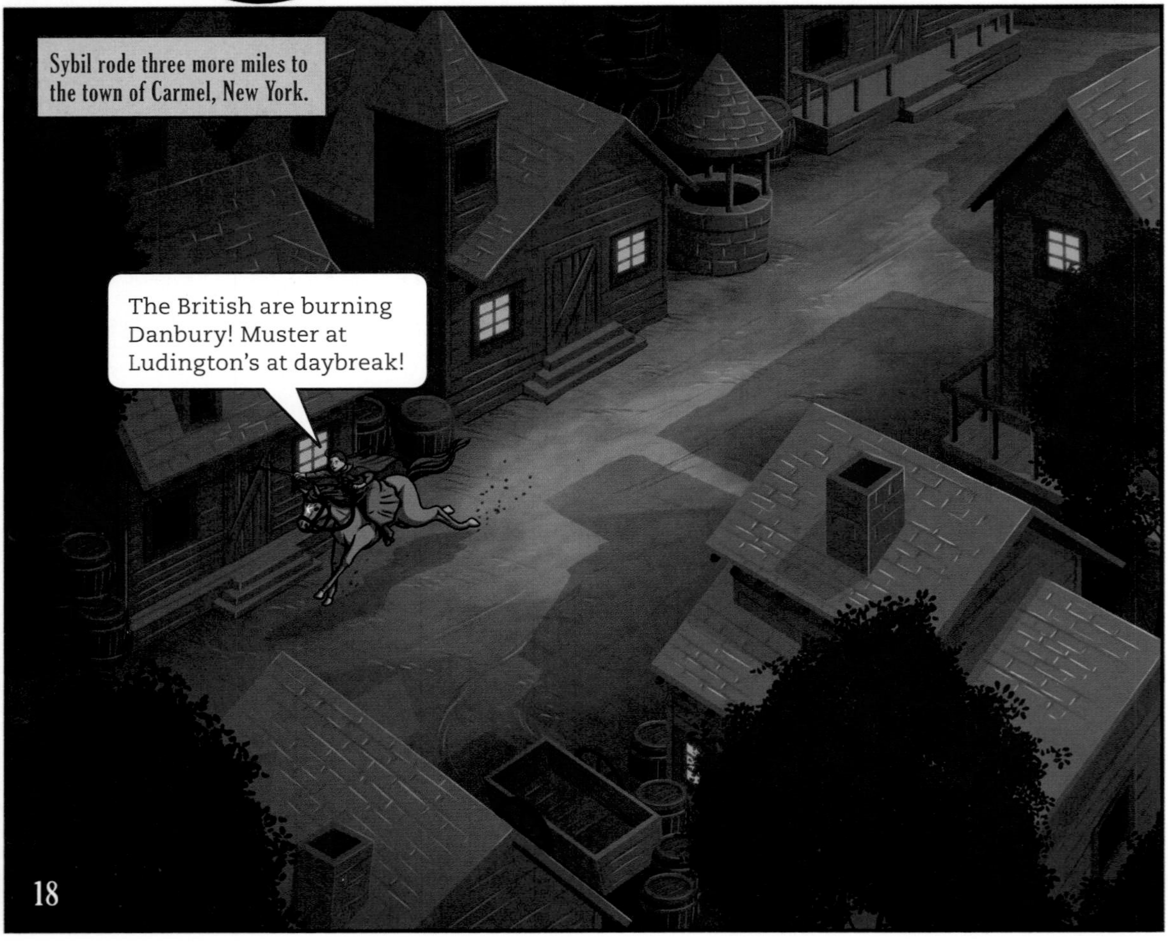
Sybil rode three more miles to the town of Carmel, New York.
The British are burning Danbury! Muster at Ludington's at daybreak!

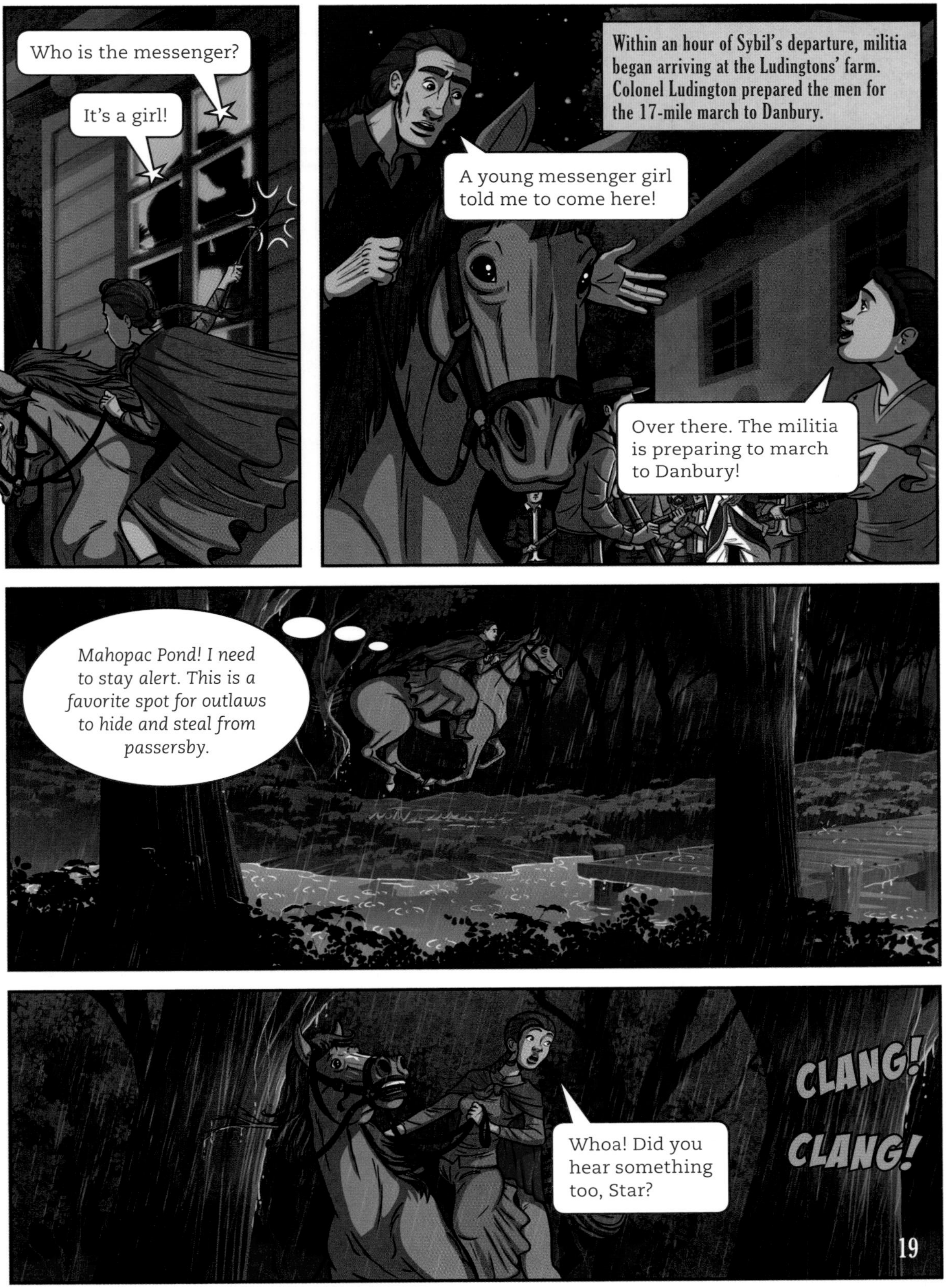
Who is the messenger?
It's a girl!
Within an hour of Sybil's departure, militia began arriving at the Ludingtons' farm. Colonel Ludington prepared the men for the 17-mile march to Danbury.
A young messenger girl told me to come here!
Over there. The militia is preparing to march to Danbury!
Mahopac Pond! I need to stay alert. This is a favorite spot for outlaws to hide and steal from passersby.
Whoa! Did you hear something too, Star?
CLANG!
CLANG!

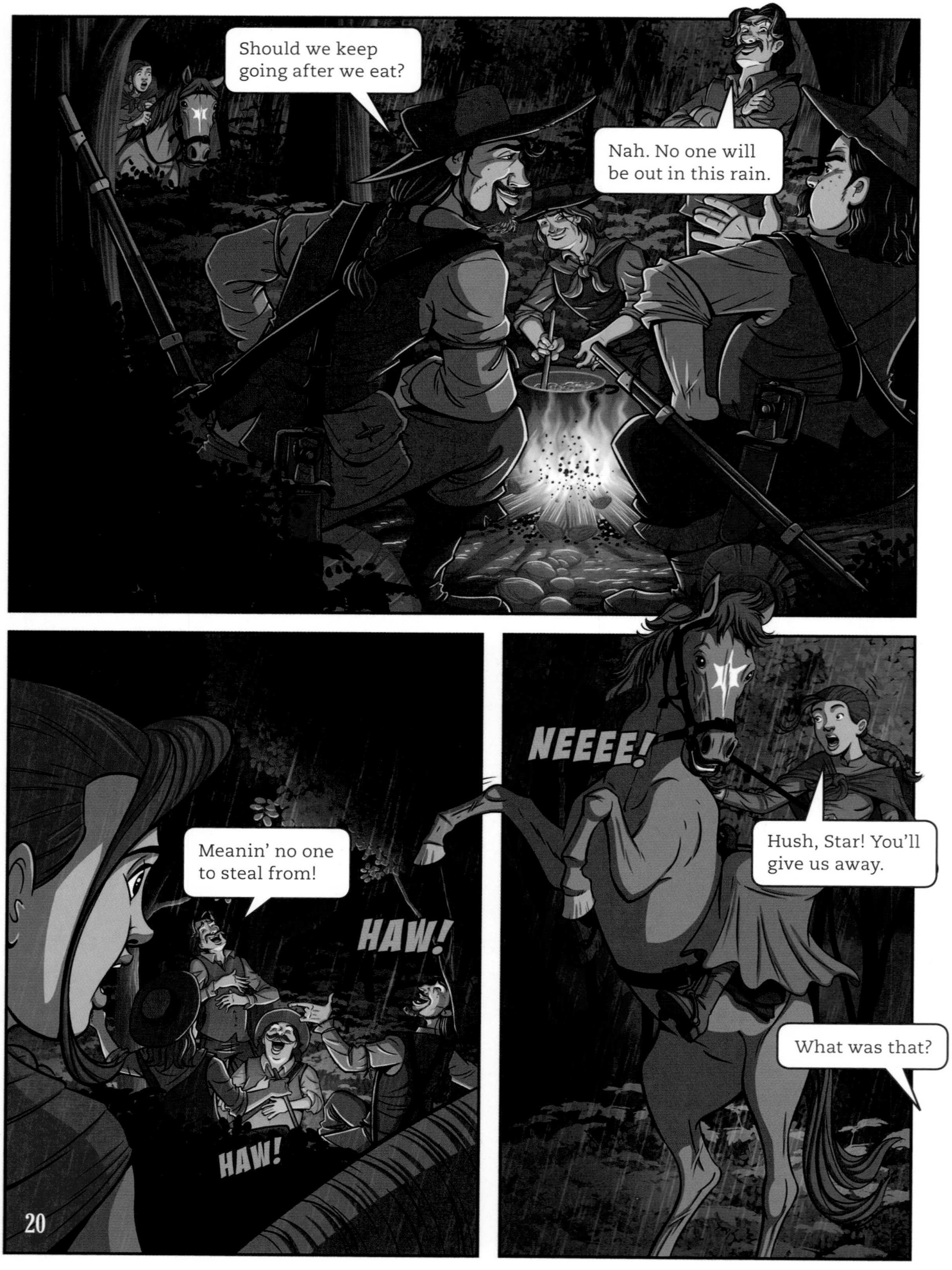
Should we keep going after we eat?
Nah. No one will be out in this rain.
Meanin' no one to steal from!
HAW!
HAW!
NEEEE!
Hush, Star! You'll give us away.
What was that?

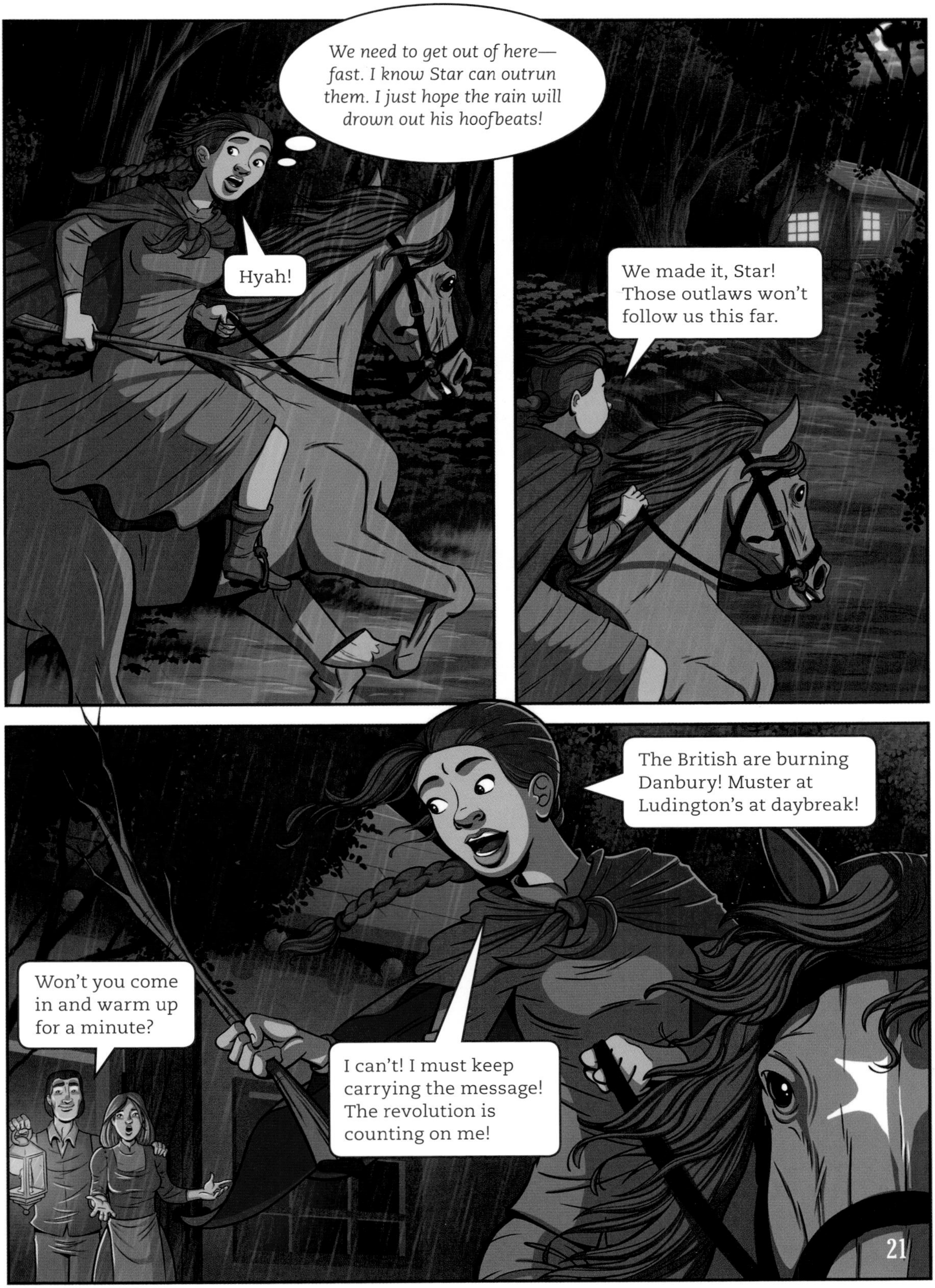
We need to get out of here—fast. I know Star can outrun them. I just hope the rain will drown out his hoofbeats!
Hyah!
We made it, Star! Those outlaws won't follow us this far.
The British are burning Danbury! Muster at Ludington's at daybreak!
Won't you come in and warm up for a minute?
I can't! I must keep carrying the message! The revolution is counting on me!

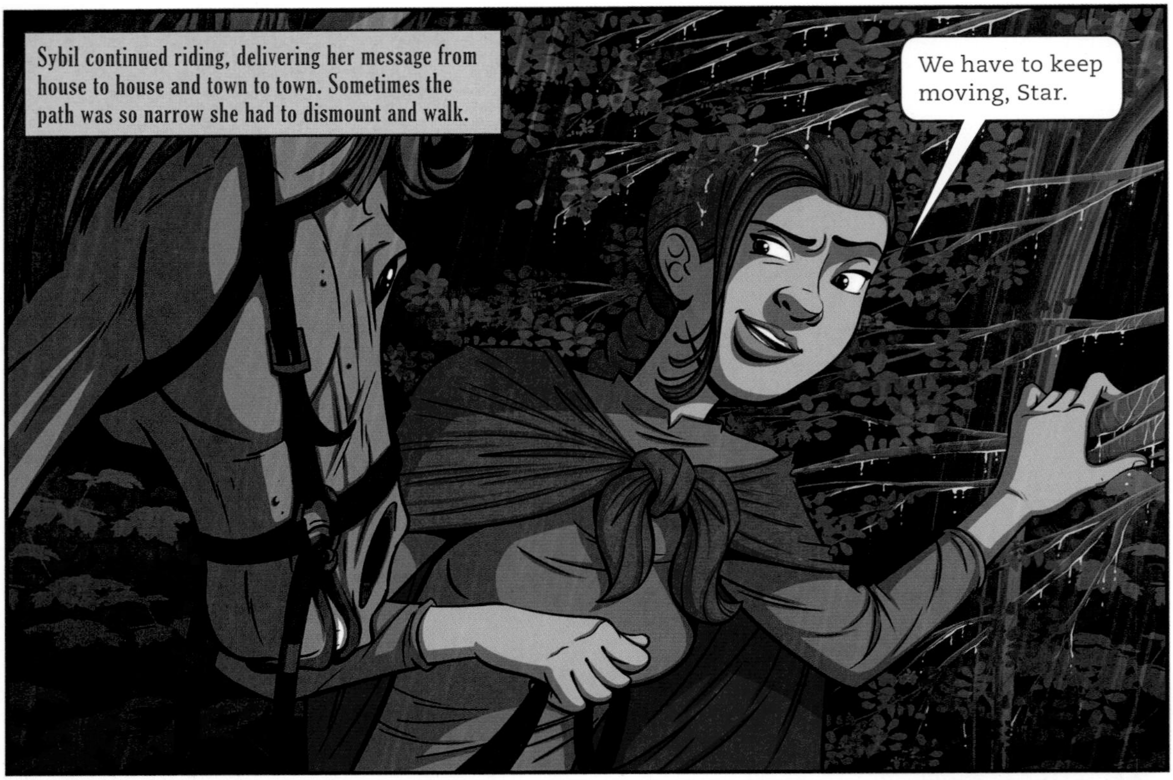
Sybil continued riding, delivering her message from house to house and town to town. Sometimes the path was so narrow she had to dismount and walk.
We have to keep moving, Star.

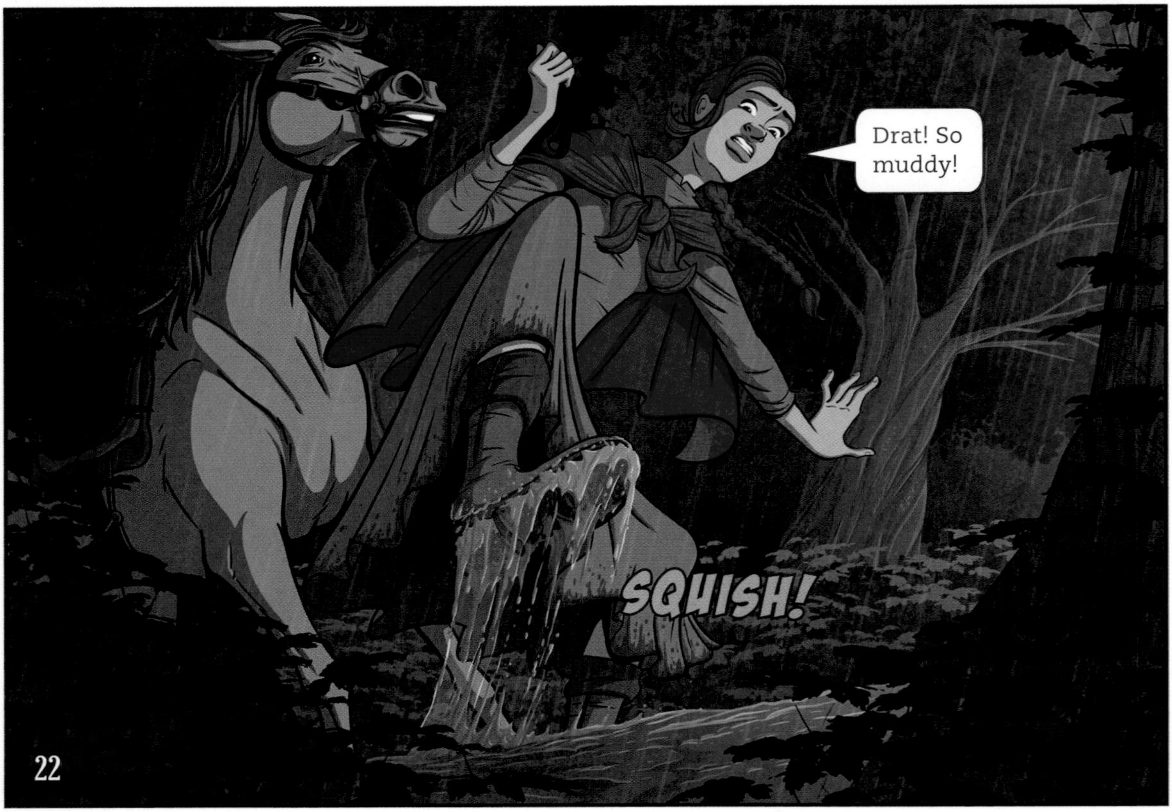
Drat! So muddy!
SQUISH!

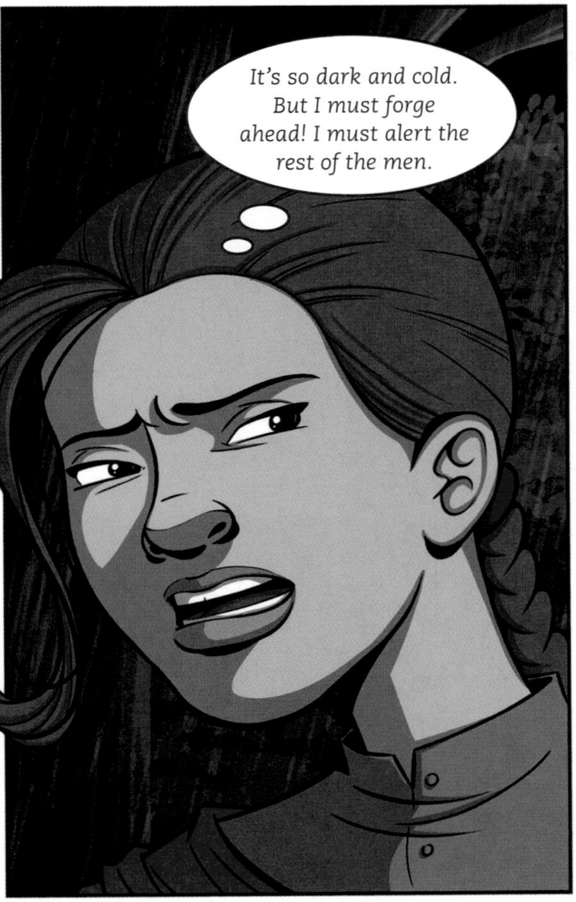

It's so dark and cold. But I must forge ahead! I must alert the rest of the men.

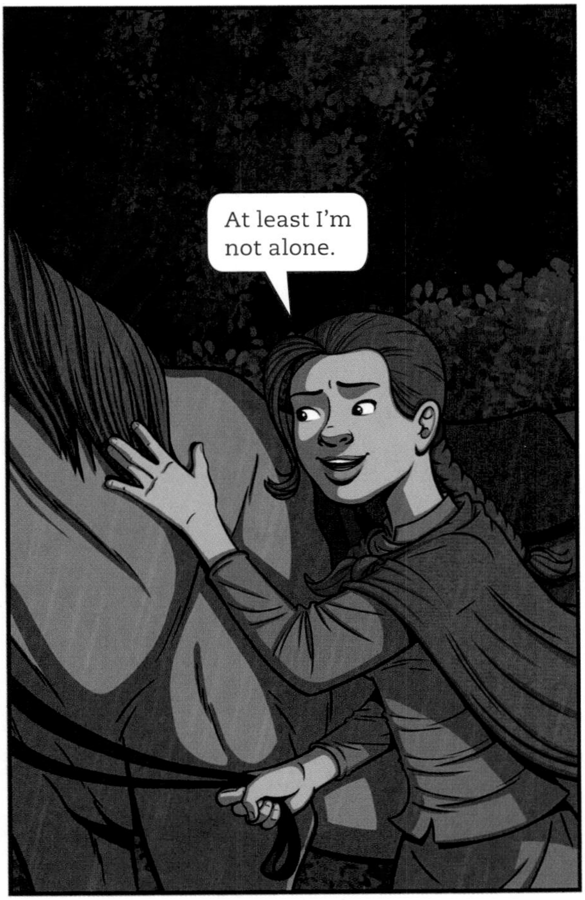

At least I'm not alone.

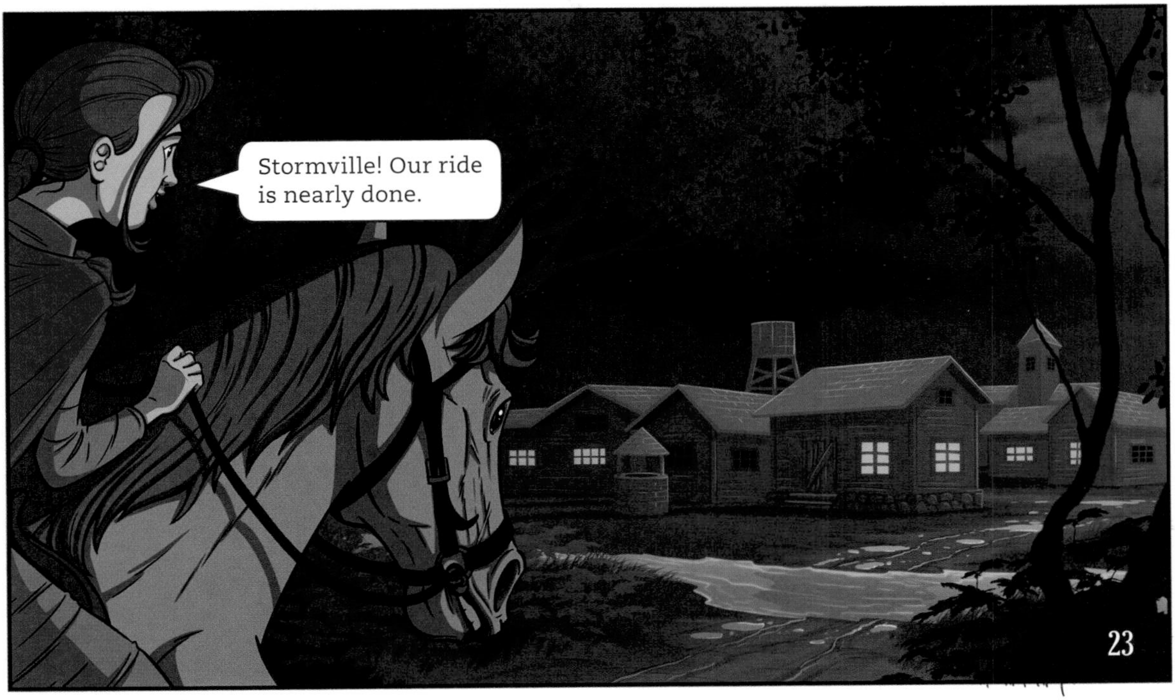

Stormville! Our ride is nearly done.

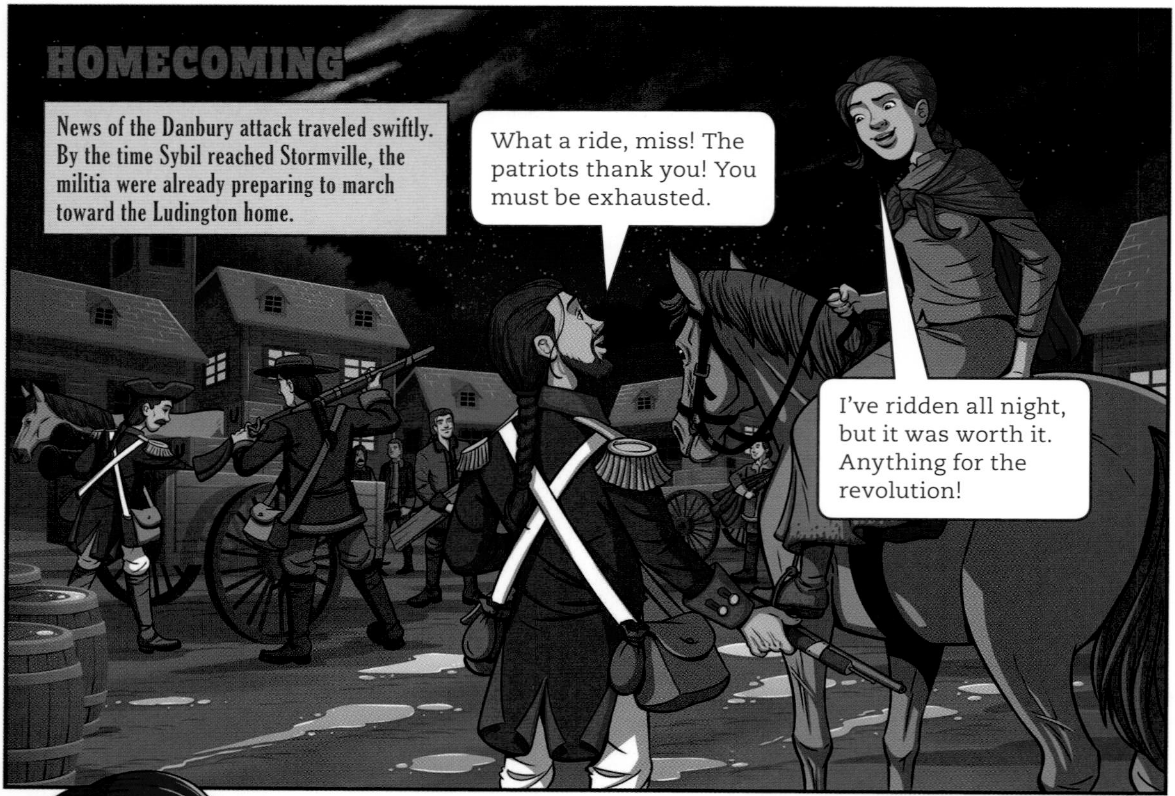
HOMECOMING
News of the Danbury attack traveled swiftly. By the time Sybil reached Stormville, the militia were already preparing to march toward the Ludington home.
What a ride, miss! The patriots thank you! You must be exhausted.
I've ridden all night, but it was worth it. Anything for the revolution!

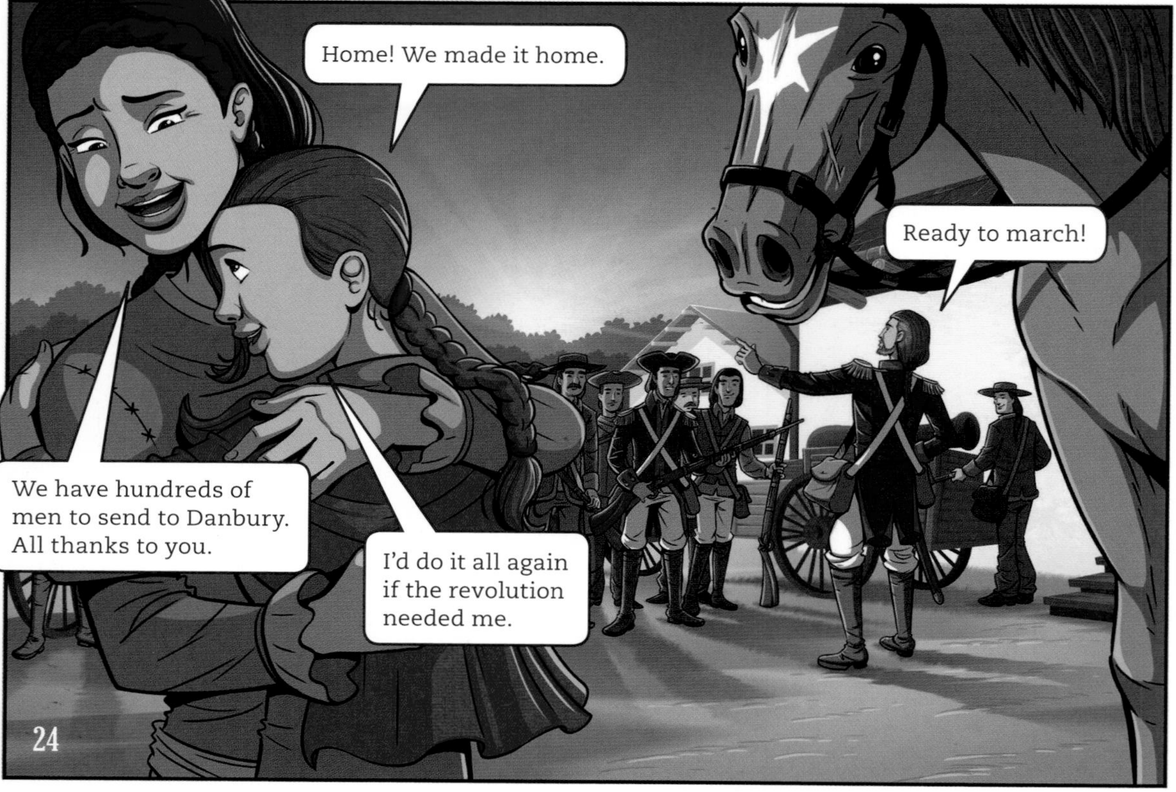
Home! We made it home.
We have hundreds of men to send to Danbury. All thanks to you.
I'd do it all again if the revolution needed me.
Ready to march!

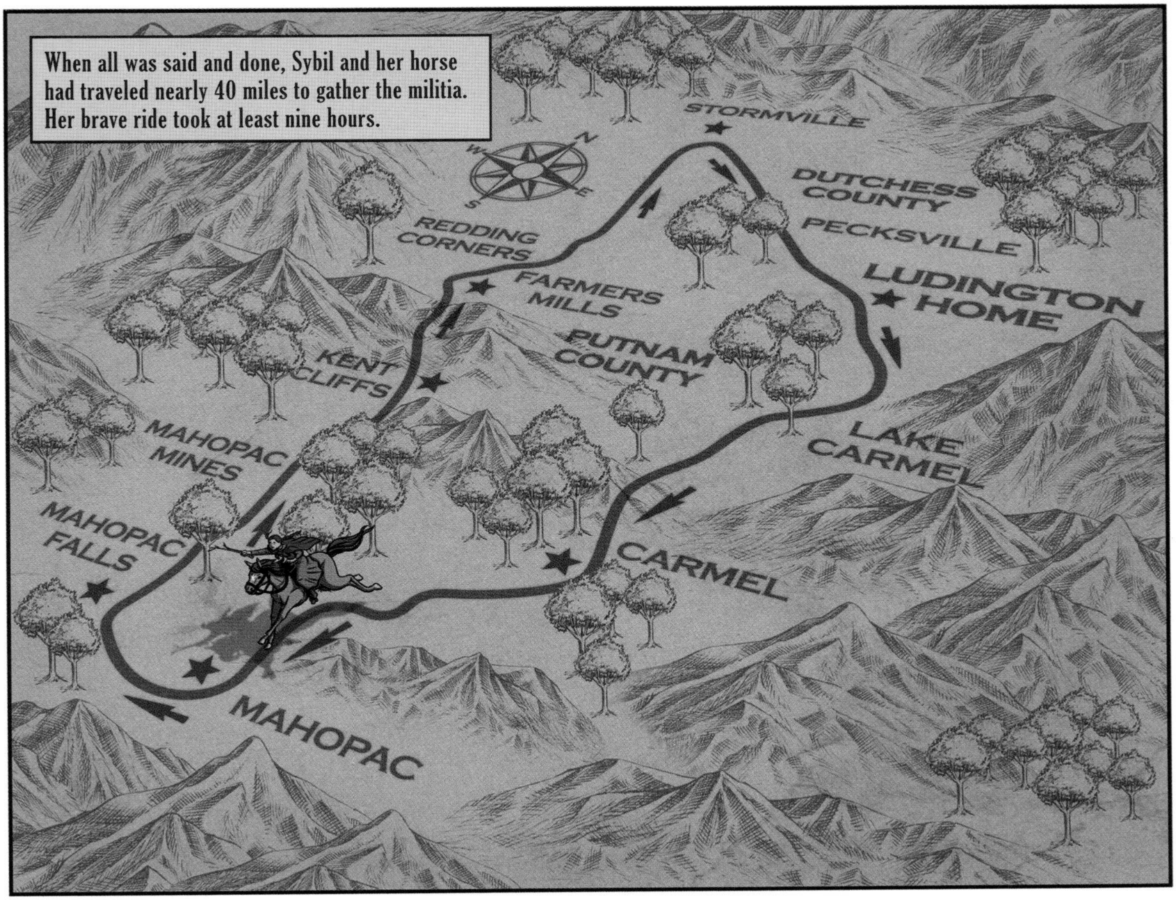
When all was said and done, Sybil and her horse had traveled nearly 40 miles to gather the militia. Her brave ride took at least nine hours.
STORMVILLE
DUTCHESS COUNTY
PECKSVILLE
REDDING CORNERS
FARMERS MILLS
LUDINGTON HOME
PUTNAM COUNTY
KENT CLIFFS
MAHOPAC MINES
LAKE CARMEL
MAHOPAC FALLS
CARMEL
MAHOPAC

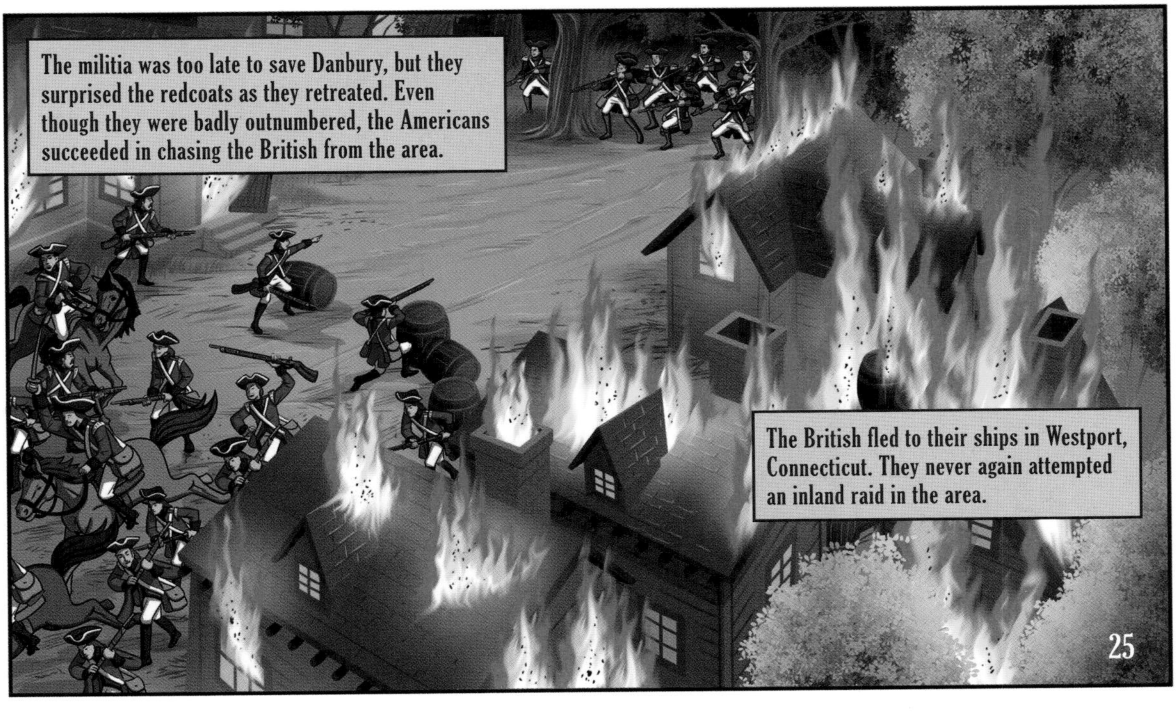
The militia was too late to save Danbury, but they surprised the redcoats as they retreated. Even though they were badly outnumbered, the Americans succeeded in chasing the British from the area.
The British fled to their ships in Westport, Connecticut. They never again attempted an inland raid in the area.

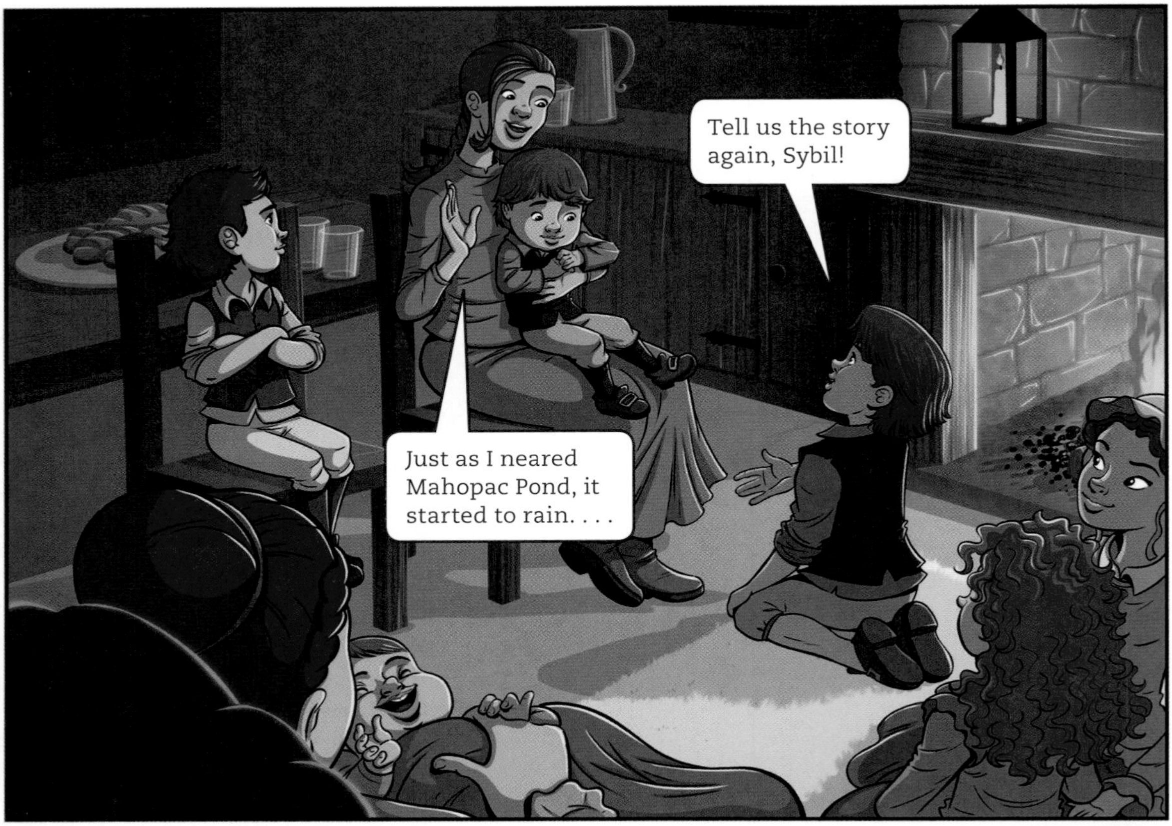
Tell us the story again, Sybil!
Just as I neared Mahopac Pond, it started to rain. . . .

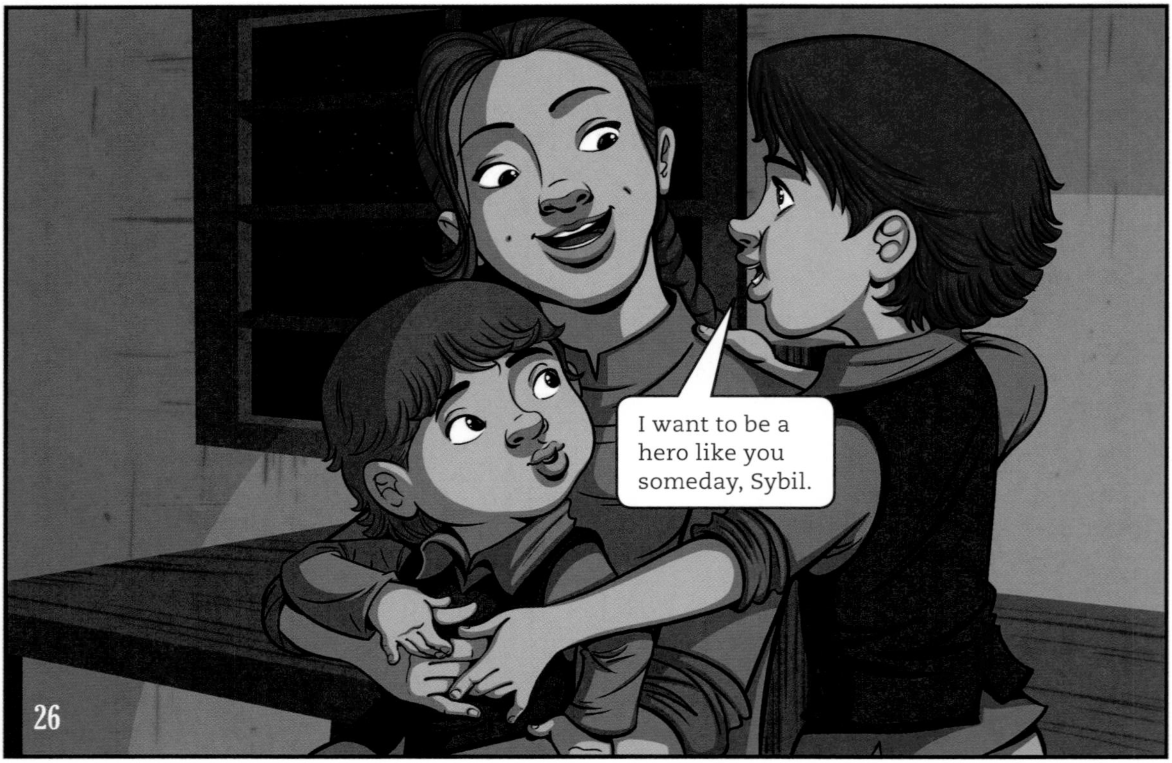
I want to be a hero like you someday, Sybil.

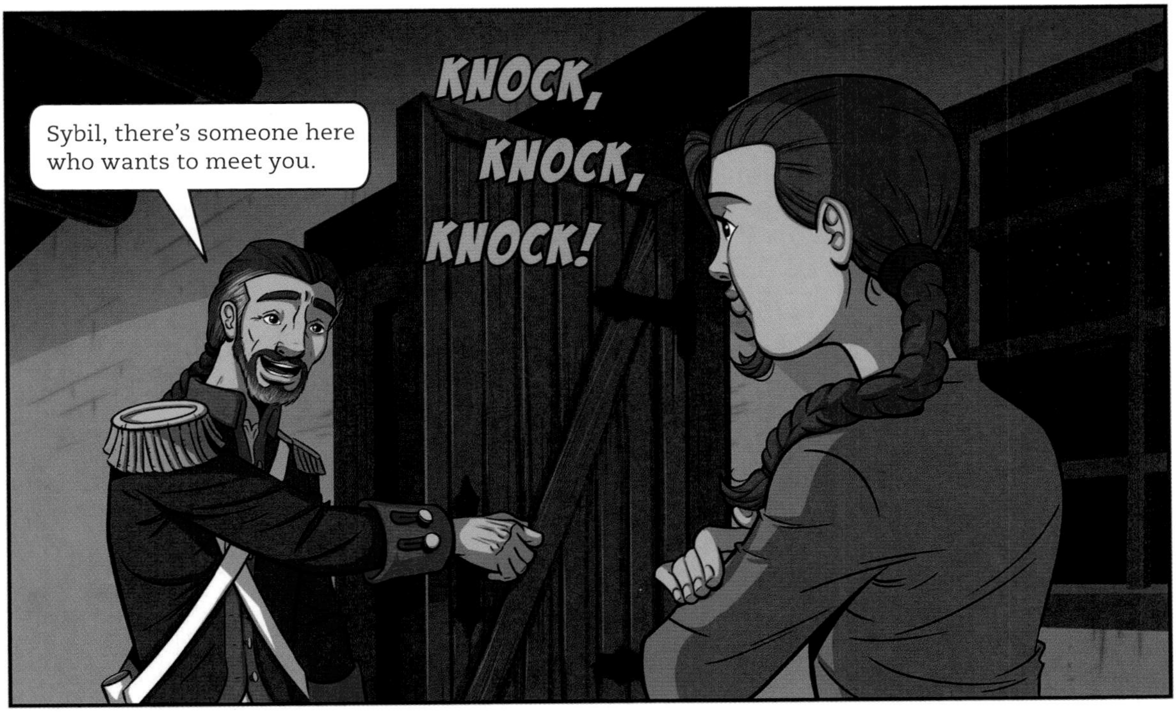
Sybil, there's someone here who wants to meet you.
KNOCK, KNOCK, KNOCK!

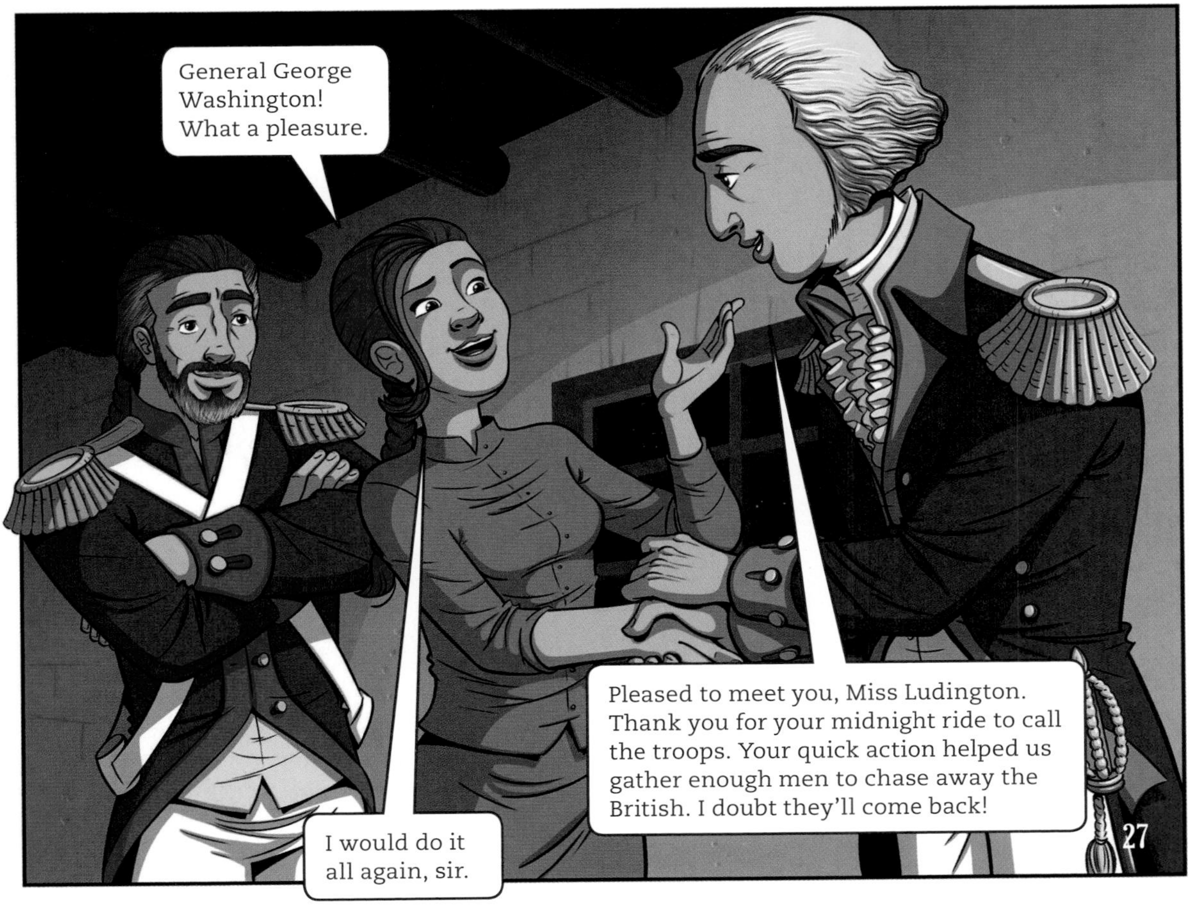
General George Washington! What a pleasure.
Pleased to meet you, Miss Ludington. Thank you for your midnight ride to call the troops. Your quick action helped us gather enough men to chase away the British. I doubt they'll come back!
I would do it all again, sir.

SYBIL LUDINGTON RIDES ON

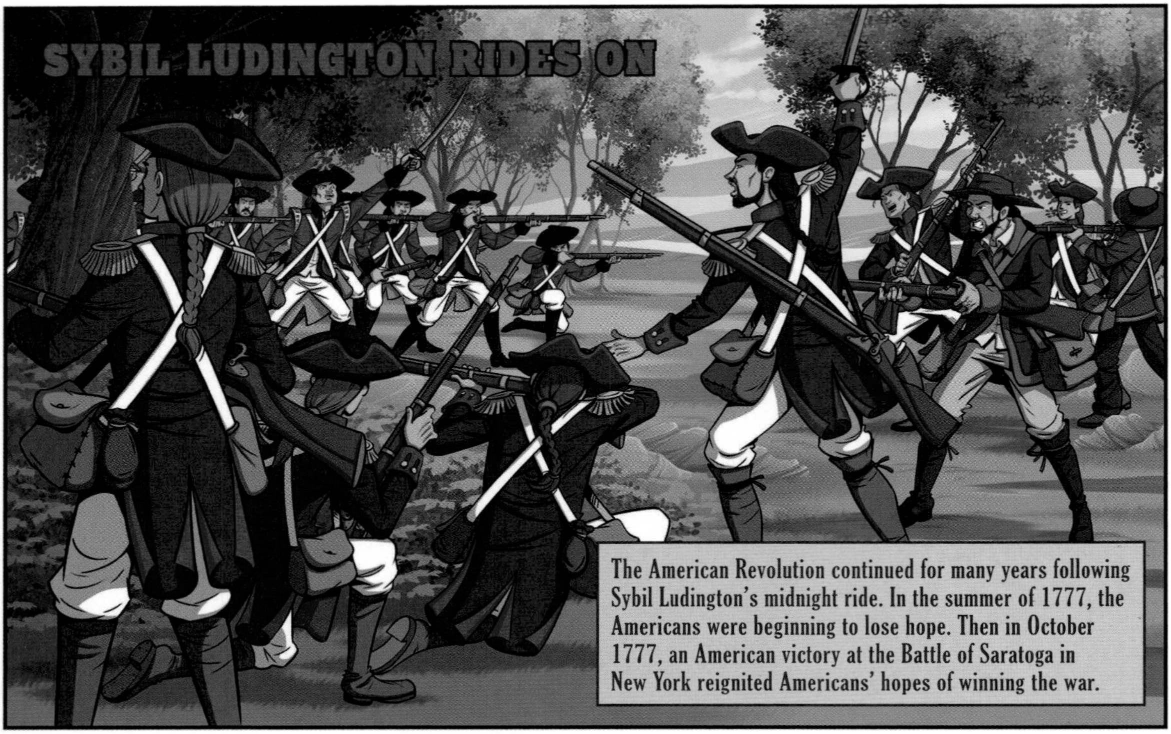
The American Revolution continued for many years following Sybil Ludington's midnight ride. In the summer of 1777, the Americans were beginning to lose hope. Then in October 1777, an American victory at the Battle of Saratoga in New York reignited Americans' hopes of winning the war.

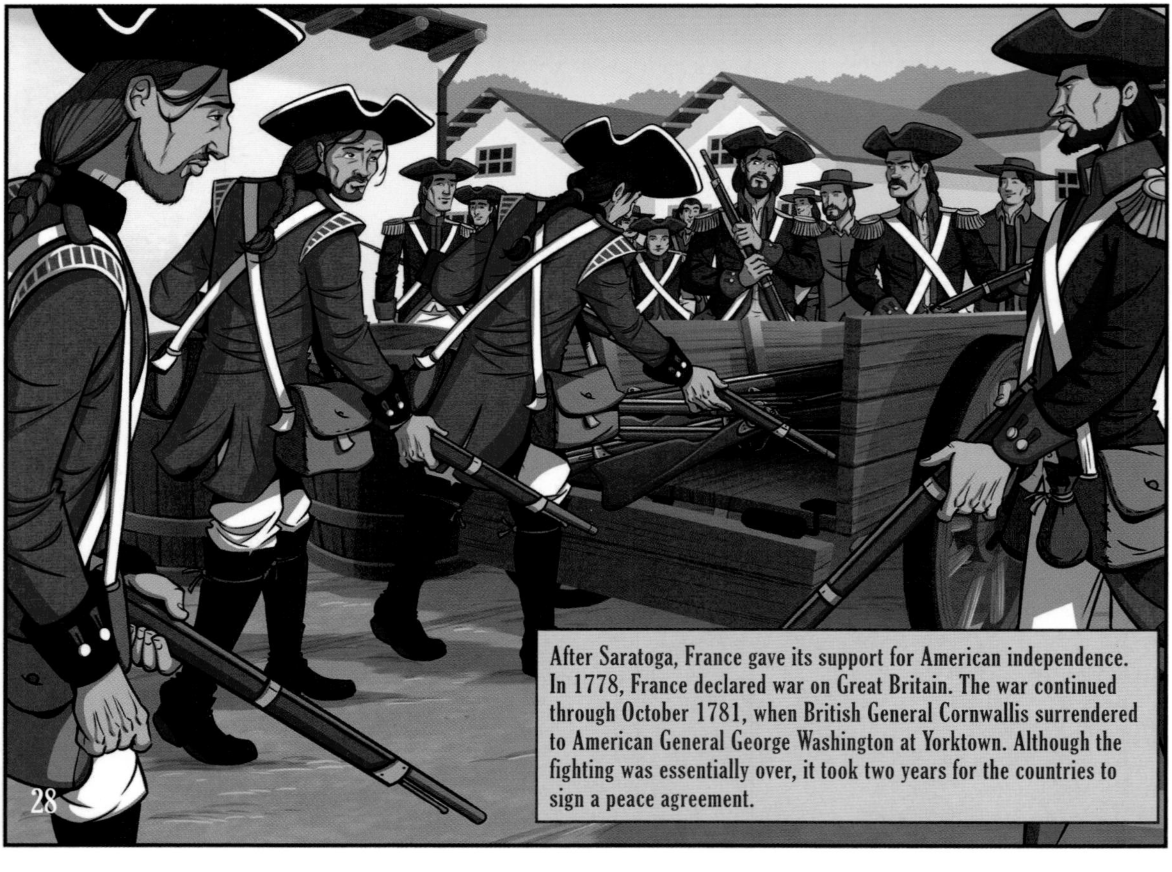
After Saratoga, France gave its support for American independence. In 1778, France declared war on Great Britain. The war continued through October 1781, when British General Cornwallis surrendered to American General George Washington at Yorktown. Although the fighting was essentially over, it took two years for the countries to sign a peace agreement.

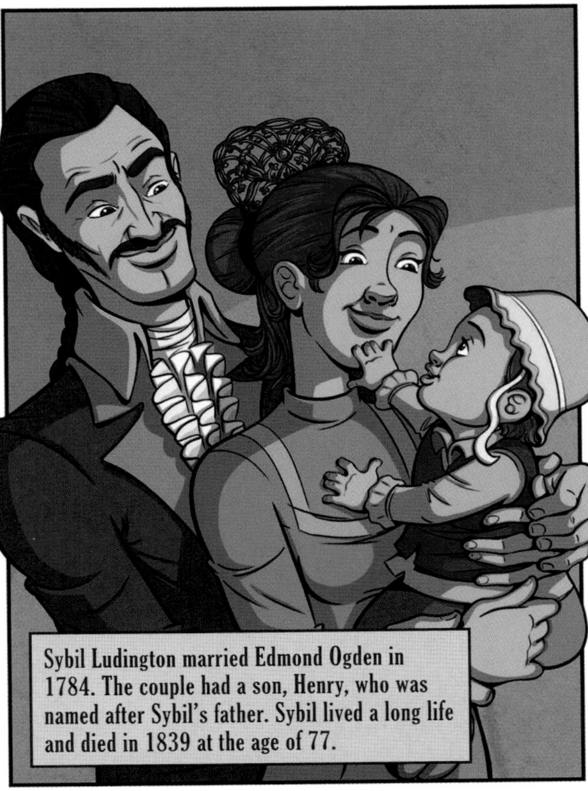
Sybil Ludington married Edmond Ogden in 1784. The couple had a son, Henry, who was named after Sybil's father. Sybil lived a long life and died in 1839 at the age of 77.

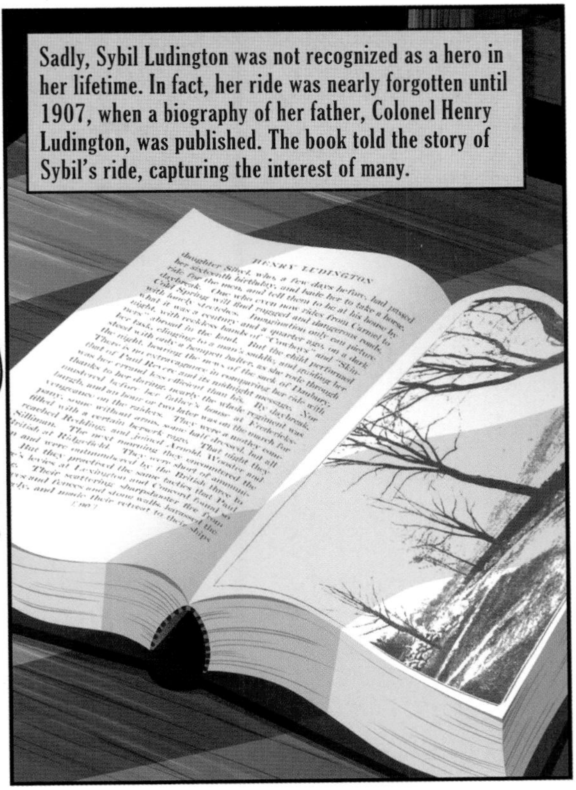
Sadly, Sybil Ludington was not recognized as a hero in her lifetime. In fact, her ride was nearly forgotten until 1907, when a biography of her father, Colonel Henry Ludington, was published. The book told the story of Sybil's ride, capturing the interest of many.

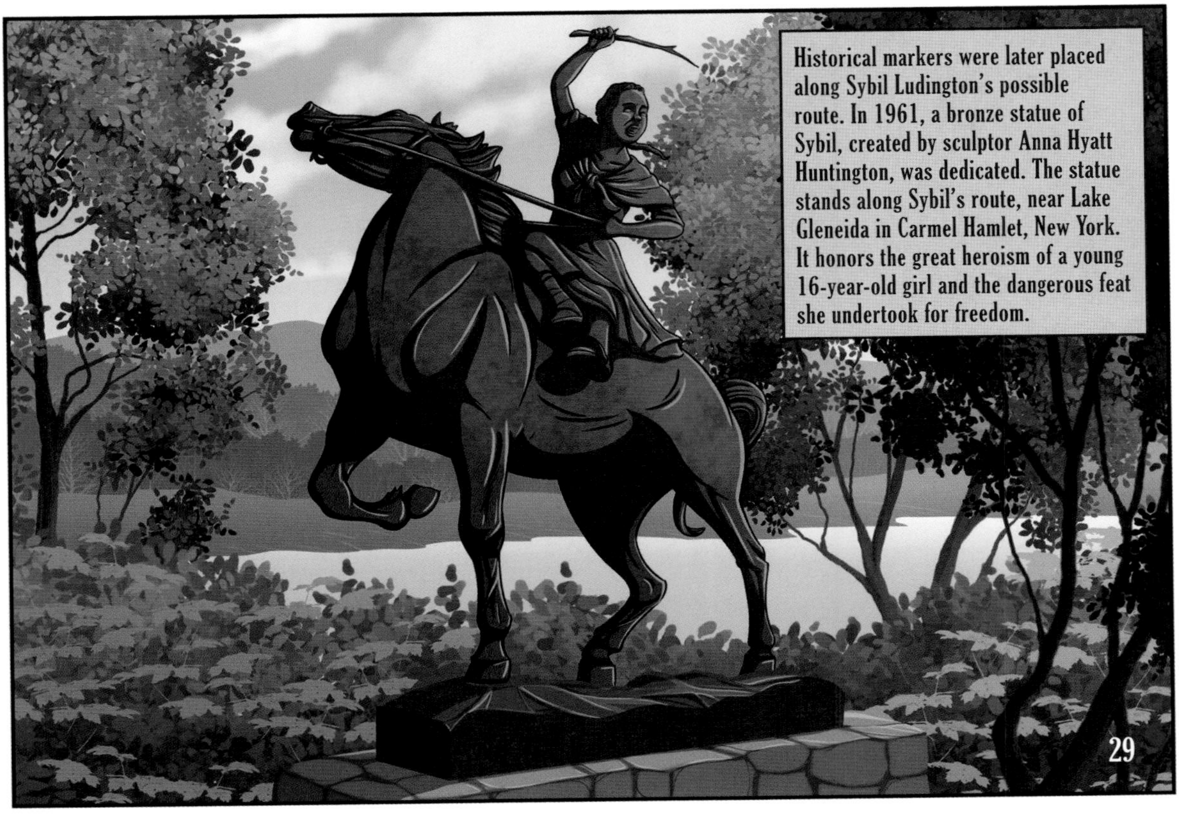
Historical markers were later placed along Sybil Ludington's possible route. In 1961, a bronze statue of Sybil, created by sculptor Anna Hyatt Huntington, was dedicated. The statue stands along Sybil's route, near Lake Gleneida in Carmel Hamlet, New York. It honors the great heroism of a young 16-year-old girl and the dangerous feat she undertook for freedom.

GLOSSARY

colonies (KAH-luh-neez)—the 13 groups of people living in North America before the Revolutionary War; they were ruled by Great Britain.

Continental Congress (kahn-tuh-nen-tuhl KAHNG-gruhs)—leaders from the 13 original American colonies who made up the American government from 1774 to 1789

forge (fohrj)—to move forward slowly but steadily

intercepted (in-tur-SEP-tid)—taken, seized, or stopped before reaching an intended destination

militia (muh-LISH-uh)—a group of volunteer citizens who serve as soldiers in emergencies

outlaw (OUT-law)—a person who has broken the law and is hiding or fleeing to avoid punishment

Parliament (PAR-luh-muhnt)—the national legislature of Great Britain

revolution (rev-uh-LOO-shuhn)—an uprising by a group of people against a system of government or a way of life

seize (SEEZ)—to take something by force

troops (TROOPS)—a group of soldiers

READ MORE

Abbott, E.F. *Sybil Ludington: Revolutionary War Rider*.
New York: Macmillan, 2016.

Amstel, Marsha. Adapted by Amanda Doering Tourville.
The Horse-Riding Adventure of Sybil Ludington, Revolutionary War Messenger. Minneapolis: Graphic Universe, 2013.

Marsico, Katie. *Sybil Ludington's Revolutionary War Story*.
Minneapolis: Lerner Publications, 2018.

INTERNET SITES

National Women's History Museum—Sybil Ludington
https://www.womenshistory.org/education-resources/
biographies/sybil-ludington

Sybil Ludington, the Teen Patriot Who Outrode Paul Revere
https://www.kidsdiscover.com/quick-reads/sybil-ludington-
teen-patriot-outrode-paul-revere/

American History for Kids—Sybil Ludington
https://www.americanhistoryforkids.com/sybil-ludington/

INDEX

American Revolution, 5, 24, 28

Battle of Lexington, 5
Battle of Quebec, 6–7
Battle of Saratoga, 28
Boston Harbor, 5
British colonies, 4
British Parliament, 4

Carmel, 18
Continental Congress, 5

Danbury, 12–13, 17–19, 21, 24–25
Declaration of Independence, 5

French and Indian War, 4, 6–7

Lake Carmel, 16
Ludington farm, 6, 8–9, 10–11, 24
Ludington, Henry, 6–8, 10–15, 27
  biography, 29
  teen years, 6–7

Ludington, Sybil
  birth, 6
  children, 29
  death, 29
  family, 26
  husband, 29
  midnight ride, 15–24, 25, 28–29

Mahopac Pond, 19, 26
militia, 5, 8, 10, 12–13, 15, 19, 24–25

outlaws, 8, 11, 14–15, 19–21

patriots, 5, 24

Revolutionary War, 5, 8

Sons of Liberty, 4–5

Stamp Act of 1765, 4

taxes, 4–5

Washington, George, 8, 27, 28